POPULAR BUDDHISM IN JAPAN
SHIN BUDDHIST RELIGION & CULTURE

Popular Buddhism in Japan

SHIN BUDDHIST RELIGION & CULTURE

Esben Andreasen

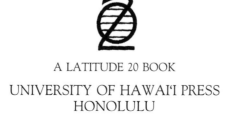

A LATITUDE 20 BOOK

UNIVERSITY OF HAWAI'I PRESS
HONOLULU

Published in North America by
University of Hawai'i Press
2840 Kolowalu Street
Honolulu, Hawai'i 96822

First published in Great Britain by
Japan Library/Curzon Press
15 The Quadrant
Richmond
Surrey TW9 1BP

Printed in England

Library of Congress Cataloguing-in-Publication Data

Andreasen, Esben
    Popular Buddhism in Japan: Shin Buddhist religion and culture/
Esben Andreasen.
      p.   cm.
    "Latitude 20 book."
    Includes bibliographical references and index.
    ISBN 0-8248-2027-4 (cloth   :   alk. paper). – ISBN 0-8248-2028-2
(pbk.   :   alk. paper)
    1.   Shin   (Sect)   I. Title.
BQ8715.4.A53   1997
294.3'926–dc21

                                            97-33209
                                              CIP

Contents

Preface

To many people in the Western world Japanese Buddhism means Zen Buddhism. The images that Zen Buddhism call up are of silent meditation halls and austere discipline. Its perceived paradoxical logic, methods and atheism have made it popular among intellectuals in the West.

For at least two reasons this Western assumption is wrong: in Japanese Buddhism Zen is a minority sect and in many respects it is not very different from other branches of Buddhism. Also among ordinary Zen Buddhists there is widespread belief in gods. Like temples in general popular Zen temples are concerned with the moral guidance of families and the performance of burials and memorial services. All traditional Buddhist sects in Japan have roots in folk religion and ancestor worship.

The dominance of Zen is easily seen in the number of books on Zen in English in the West and in Japanese bookshops catering for Western tourists. The great popularizer of Japanese Buddhism, D.T. Suzuki, is mainly known as a Zen Buddhist, but in reality he also wrote books on Shin Buddhism. But they have not met the same demand. When the famous Japanese journal in English, *The Eastern Buddhist*, was first published in 1921 with Suzuki as one of the editors, the purpose was to transmit both Zen and Shin to the West, but in time Zen took over. The fact is that Shin Buddhism has considerably more followers than Zen – even in the USA where immigrants who came to work on plantations and farms came from agricultural areas in Japan with strong connections to Shin Buddhism. The popularity of Zen in the USA, therefore, belongs to a different class of people, the more educated and intellectual. But also Shin Buddhism is 'a major contribution' to Japanese culture, to quote D.T. Suzuki.

This introduction to Shin Buddhism in the form of a textbook originates from a wish I had in 1989 when I first visited Otani University, Kyoto, as a member of a European study tour. I realized that this more popular form of Buddhism was a neglected field in Western studies on Japanese religions. Subsequently, in the autumn of 1992, I was accepted as a visiting researcher at Otani University for six months with the intention of preparing an annotated description of Shin Buddhism through the use of a variety of extant texts.

In this book I have chosen to focus on religious practice and to a lesser extent I have selected material illustrating the theology of Shin Buddhism. This is partly to reflect my own understanding of what is most important, and partly due to the fact that religion in Japan is a matter of tradition and ritual, less a matter of formalized dogmatics.

Thus, the contents include the history of Shin Buddhism, especially the founder Shinran and the modern age, and the rituals of the religion. In addition, there are chapters on the influence of Shin Buddhism on arts and crafts, on Shin Buddhist education, and a chapter on Shin Buddhism in Hawai'i seen from the point of view of culture clash. Texts with no author attribution are written by me and are mainly descriptions of ceremonies or interviews.

I wish to thank my advisers at Otani University: Professor Minoru Tada, my senior adviser, and Professor Yasutomi Shinya, who also acted as my interpreter and invited me to participate in the Ho-onko at his father's temple. Also President Terakawa Shunsho, Dean Furuta Kazuhiro and Dean Minoura Eryo. Likewise, the administration at Higashi Honganji, especially Rev. Fujii Shoryo, who was my link with the head temple. Moreover, I wish to thank Rev. Dennis Hirota, Hongwanji International Center, who I am especially grateful for suggestions and texts regarding Shin Buddhism and the arts of Japan. Finally, I would like to thank Lecturer Higuchi Shoshin, my travelling companion to Hawai'i, and Mr Kamata Tetsuo, who travelled with me to Toyama – both from Otani University. For his invaluable help in editing the book and for writing a Foreword and Postscript I wish to thank Professor Alfred Bloom wholeheartedly. Any shortcomings or inaccuracies that may be found in the book are entirely my responsibility.

According to Japanese custom, all Japanese names appear with family names first.

ESBEN ANDREASEN

Foreword

The field of Pure Land Studies and Jodo Shin Buddhism, in particular, has begun increasingly to attract interest among scholars of religion, theologians and ordinary people, because it combines a highly developed symbol system, a devotional focus and philosophic, reflective thought. Once considered by foreign observers as a debased, popular form of Buddhism because of its mass appeal, more recent and accurate research has shown that its exponents may be critical thinkers, as well as committed followers, and that its insights into the human condition should not be underestimated merely because of its reputation as one of the largest Buddhist denominations in Japan.

In the present text, the author makes a significant contribution to our knowledge of the Shin Buddhist faith by bringing together a variety of resources which offer insight into such diverse dimensions of the tradition as documents from its early beginnings, examples of modern interpretation, and representative pieces on cultural, religious and organizational life. The text goes beyond merely doctrinal considerations, enabling the reader to gain a broad perspective on the contemporary situation of the sect.

Mr Andreasen is to be commended for his diligence in filling a need in Shin Buddhist studies with his anthology of historical and contemporary resources of Shin Buddhism, not all easily available to Western students. His text will enable a deeper study of this significant strand of Japanese Buddhism.

ALFRED BLOOM
Professor Emeritus
Department of Religion
University of Hawai'i

List of Illustrations

Gautama and Amitabha (Nison-in, Kyoto)

Meeting Popular Buddhism in Japan

The threads of life are mysterious. My own experience is a case in point. Why did I become so engulfed in Buddhism and how did it happen that I came to like Japanese Shin Buddhism in particular?

My life has been quite ordinary. I studied English and Religious Studies at Copenhagen University, planning to teach high school once I obtained my degree. My first memorable encounter with Buddhism was in 1970 as a first-year teacher on a field-trip with my high school students. We attended an exhibition called 'The Ways of Buddha' at the Danish National Museum. My initial impressions were quite strong. I clearly felt the mildness, lenience and tolerance that radiated from the exhibits, especially those of the historical Buddha. The exhibition catalogue still sits on my bookshelf allowing me to recall the vivid scenes of Buddha from Sri Lanka, India, Tibet, Nepal, Mongolia, China and Japan. Even so my early impressions and understanding were still quite general – as was my teaching of Buddha in the classroom. I taught from the classic texts of Theravada Buddhism, as is the tradition within Western European Buddhist scholarship.

In 1982 I was invited by the Japanese Ministry of Education to participate in a study-tour of Japanese education. I jumped at the opportunity and spent the bulk of my time carrying out the mission of the visit by comparing the Danish and Japanese schools systems. However, I used every free moment visiting, wandering through, and photographing gardens, temples and shrines to increase my understanding of Japanese culture and history. I returned from that trip in awe of the country, its people, and their cultural traditions. I began reading a frenzy of books on Japan that continues today. And I began to understand the role of religion in

Japanese life.

A year later, I took a class to another exhibit at the Danish National Museum – this one was called simply 'Japan'. The catalogue accompanying the exhibit was filled with four-colour photos of Zen gardens, ornate yet simple shrines, and the ritual of the Japanese tea ceremony. My teaching of Buddhism moved to a new level as I assembled the photographic slides I took the previous year in Japan into a slide-lecture programme. The students and I studied Zen texts, using the slides to visually enhance our understanding of Japanese Buddhism.

Eventually, the slides developed into a published slide series on Japanese religions and was sold throughout Denmark. I then co-edited in the Danish language the first book-length textbook on Japanese religions. The book was subsequently translated into English, further edited and improved by the noted Japanese religions scholar Ian Reader. The book was published to much acclaim by the Japan Library in England and the University of Hawai'i Press in the United States under the title, *Japanese Religions: Past and Present*. Now a standard text in religious studies courses, the book focuses almost entirely on Japanese Zen Buddhism.

My continuing studies into Japanese religions have introduced me to many forms of Japanese Buddhism other than Zen. In fact, my second Danish language textbook on Japanese religions intentionally excluded Zen. The book introduces readers to Shin Buddhism, Shugendo, and New Religions, among other subjects. My co-editors and I wanted to introduce Westerners to Pure Land Buddhism in particular. The book, *Japan: Religion and Life Styles*, is the outgrowth of research conducted at several religious sites in Kyoto. We found in these Shin Buddhist circles a religious attitude which combined seriousness with a modern outlook, together with an openness and friendliness towards those new to the religion. This was Buddhism in the midst of life, practised by people from many different backgrounds, with no pretensions whatsoever. These encounters were quite refreshing.

Following the publication of the second book, I found that I was still in need of a deeper understanding of Buddhism as a living religion. I wanted to move from the general to the specific. I felt I must return to Japan to do this, so I applied for and received a grant to study Shin Buddhism as a visiting researcher at Otani University in Kyoto. For six months I talked daily with Shin Buddhists, at temples and in their homes. I also joined a group that went to Hawai'i to spend time with active Shin congregations.

My Buddhist education has become broader and my knowledge deeper. Interestingly, my first impression of Buddhism all those years ago at the exhibition on 'The Ways of Buddha' remains the most important: mildness, lenience, and tolerance are the cornerstones of coming to an understanding of Shin Buddhism. I cannot recall a time when my Shin Buddhist friends spoke ill of anyone. For example, during group discussions I would on occasion become quite impatient with a member of the group and turn to another for help. While this might have been acceptable in Western academic circles, it clearly was beyond the understanding of Shin Buddhists. Typically, the Shin Buddhist I turned to for help would indeed come to my assistance and the person would then heap praise on the person I had unintentionally treated rudely. I found this gentleness of spirit in all of my dealings with Shin Buddhists. It is a way of life, a way of thinking that is true to its religious tradition.

I have spent quite some time now studying Buddhism, yet no one has ever asked me to become a Buddhist. On the contrary, during discussions on religious beliefs I was expected to be the standard-bearer for Christian beliefs. Apparently, my efforts were seen as half-hearted as I did not convince too many Buddhists that I was strongly Christian in my thinking. However, my keen interest in Buddhism and religion was to them proof that I had a 'religious heart' and that it did not matter what religion I practised. They, in turn, opened their hearts and minds to me so that I could better explain to others the basic tenets of Shin Buddhism. The book is one attempt to make Shin Buddhist beliefs more widely known and understood.

Through the selected readings and what I have written I hope I have conveyed to the reader my deep commitment to the values underlying the Shin Buddhist experience. Before turning to the readings, however, Part II of this General Introduction takes a look at how Shin Buddhism evolved – in other words the development of Mahayana Buddhism itself.

The Development of Mahayana Buddhism

The two main branches of Buddhism today are *Theravada* ('the doctrine of the elders') and *Mahayana* ('the large vehicle'). When the split occurred and why are not fully explained. Traditionally, Theravada is looked upon as a continuation of early Buddhism with the monastic order at its centre, whereas Mahayana becomes a popular development in which lay followers are taught the liberation or enlightenment of all. But many scholars doubt that there was only one kind of Buddhism before Mahayana. They see Mahayana as a broad river of new ideas overflowing into various types of Buddhism. To complicate matters: in some forms of Mahayana the followers also had a kind of monastic initiation, and also early Buddhism had elements of *stupa* worship, a characteristic normally attributed to Mahayana. (A stupa is a Buddhist reliquary, originally a burial mound.)

The date of the first Mahayana sutras (holy Buddhist writings) is the first century BC, and the development of Mahayana culminates in about the seventh and eighth centuries AD. The region where the development took place is still the native country of Buddhism – the northern part of India.

MAIN FEATURES OF MAHAYANA BUDDHISM

One very important element in Mahayana Buddhism is the *bodhisattva*, that is the one who postpones his final complete enlightenment and attainment of nirvana in order to help all other beings in their quest for enlightenment. Such a bodhisattva is involved with works of supererogation which benefit the believers who pray to the bodhisattva.

Mahayana is a religion with many developed forms of religious practice, among which meditation, the recitation of sutras and the employment of magic. The use of the power reached through meditation is especially important. And both bodhisattvas and sutras are magical centres of power. Mahayana Buddhism accepts a plurality of buddhas and bodhisattvas, both of which are divine and have supernatural power.

But also all sentient beings contain a Buddha nature and may reach buddhahood. It is typical of Mahayana Buddhism to make use of bodhisattva vows, which are promises not to enter nirvana and final buddhahood before all people who believe in them are liberated.

On top of this the philosophical school in Mahayana, *Madhyamika*, used arguments which were to be of great importance for the breaking down of the distinctions between monks and laity. One principle is that all things in the cosmos lack the ability to be totally independent and so are empty (*sunyata*). Even samsara and nirvana are co-dependent, because what is relative is dependent on what is absolute. Another argument is that you cannot reach nirvana by force of will, because craving after non-craving (nirvana) is also craving. To strive for nirvana turns nirvana into samsara, the ordinary world of birth and death. So it is possible to maintain that nirvana and samsara are one and the same. One of the consequences is that to lead an ordinary family life is legitimate, and that the Buddhism of the laity is considered as valuable as the Buddhism of the monks. It should be added that this development allowed Buddhism to absorb important moral values in China and Japan, such as 'filial piety' and the primacy of the family.

DEVELOPMENTS IN CHINESE BUDDHISM

Buddhism came to China via merchants travelling on the Silk Road or sailing from India to China. It was introduced around the beginning of the first century AD.

It was Mahayana Buddhism especially which came to dominate in China. Besides the above-mentioned philosophical school, Madhyamika, founded in India about 200 AD, three main streams should be mentioned: *Ch'an* Buddhism, *Cheng-yen* Buddhism and Pure Land Buddhism, the latter being the branch leading up to Shin Buddhism.

Ch'an Buddhism can be traced to India, but developed in China. Ch'an means 'meditation', and the school emphasizes that human beings can free themselves by means of meditation through

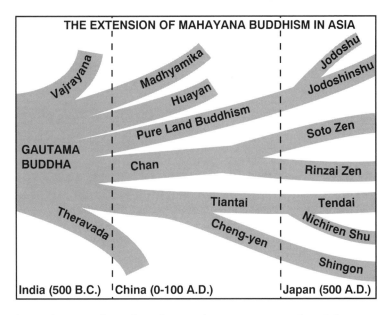

THE EXTENSION OF MAHAYANA BUDDHISM IN ASIA

Vajrayana

Madhyamika

Huayan

Jodoshu

Jodoshinshu

GAUTAMA BUDDHA

Pure Land Buddhism

Soto Zen

Chan

Rinzai Zen

Tiantai

Tendai

Theravada

Cheng-yen

Nichiren Shu

Shingon

India (500 B.C.) | China (0-100 A.D.) | Japan (500 A.D.)

the realization that all and everything is connected and form one whole. Ch'an reached Japan a few centuries later where it is called Zen Buddhism, Zen being Japanese for meditation.

Cheng-yen is esoteric Buddhism which means 'Buddhism for the initiated only'. The concept covers a range of independent developments which all worship *Vairocana*, the cosmic Buddha. Extensive use is made of magical means, such as *mantra* ('holy formula'), *mandala* ('symbolic picture of the universe') and *mudra* ('symbolic gesture of the hand and fingers'). In Japan, Cheng-yen developed into *Shingon* Buddhism. Shingon came to influence another main school in Japan, *Tendai* from the Chinese *T'ien-t'ai*, which holds the *Lotus sutra* in the place of honour. It contains the classic Mahayana argument that the historical Gautama Buddha withheld the Mahayana teachings for coming generations, as his contemporaries were not fit to receive the true teaching. Tendai is the dominating form of Buddhism at the time when Shin Buddhism becomes an independent Buddhist sect. Tendai's theory of the history of Buddhism lies behind most forms of Japanese Buddhism as all major founders of Japanese Buddhist sects studied at Mount Hiei, the main Tendai complex of temples north-east of Kyoto.

Pure Land Buddhism will receive special treatment below, as it is the main branch of Buddhism from which Shin Buddhism stems. Also in China it was immensely popular centring on *Omit'o*

Buddha, which is Chinese for sanskrit *Amitabha* Buddha, and who is the equivalent of *Amida* Buddha in Japanese Buddhism. (Amitabha means 'infinite life' and 'infinite light' in sanskrit.) The Pure Land (*sukhavati*) is the name of the paradisal place for those who are saved.

AMIDA BUDDHISM

B riefly told, Amida Buddhism is the form of Mahayana Buddhism in which the invocation of the name of Amida Buddha and the belief in Amida Buddha's power to save human beings is taught.

Probably Amida Buddhism arose among laymen, and its sutras were written between 200 and 350 AD in Gandhara, the Buddhist kingdom located on the trade routes in present-day Pakistan and Afghanistan by the upper reaches of the Indus river.

According to Buddhist sutras, Amida was born as a king and became a mendicant monk with the name Dharmakara. (His life story much resembles that of Gautama Buddha.) Out of compassion for mankind he set up 48 vows or conditions before entering nirvana. This was granted. Among the vows the most important is the 18th vow:

> If, when I attain Buddhahood, the sentient beings of the ten quarters, with sincere mind entrusting them-selves, aspiring to be born in my land, and saying my Name even ten times, should not be born there, may I not attain the supreme enlightenment. Excluded are those who commit the five grave offences, and those who slander the right dharma.
>
> (*Sukhavati-vyuha-sutra*)

'Name' refers to *nembutsu* ('Namu Amida Butsu' homage to Amida Buddha) and originally one was meant to think of or to contemplate Amida, but with time it came to be understood as an invocation of the name of Amida.

DEVELOPMENTS IN JAPANESE BUDDHISM

B uddhism came to Japan in the middle of the sixth century together with other Chinese forms of culture. According to *Nihongi*, the ancient chronicles of Japan from 720 AD, a Buddha

Amida-raigo-zazo (Musée Guimet, Paris)

statue and some sutras were sent to the Japanese Emperor from a Korean King. It can also be seen from old sources that around this time Buddhist death masses were performed at court. After some years of competition with the indigenous Japanese religion, *Shinto*, Buddhism established itself. In 604, Prince Shotoku, the de facto ruler of the country, in his '17 Articles', which formed the basic principles of a constitution, revered Buddhism as the foundation of morality.

Still, for quite some time Buddhism remained a religion for the Imperial Family, the nobility and the highest classes in society. In the Heian Period (794-1185), however, Amida Buddhism came to Japan, but it was not until the Kamakura Period (1185-1333) that popular Buddhism spread in Japan. The two main sects of Amida Buddhism, *Jodoshu* and *Jodoshinshu*, belong to this period of Japanese history in which the warrior class became the ruling class.

JODOSHU

J odo is Japanese for 'The Pure Land' and *shu* means sect. This first independent form of Amida Buddhism in Japan was founded by *Honen* (1133-1212). He got his religious education as a Tendai monk and scholar on Mount Hiei outside Kyoto. After his break with the dominant Tendai school, he established himself in Kyoto, had Shinran and other important religious persons among his followers, but was banned and had to go into exile when the established forms of Buddhism persuaded the authorities to prohibit the new teaching. The prohibition is also called the *nembutsu*-ban, because the new popular forms of Buddhism preached the recitation of the prayer *Namu Amida Butsu*. In early Amida Buddhism, saying *nembutsu* was considered sufficient for salvation, but later, in Shin Buddhism, it is looked upon as the result of the workings of Amida in the believer.

SHIN BUDDHISM OR JODOSHINSHU

T he Japanese name for Shin Buddhism is *Jodoshinshu*, 'The True Pure Land Religion', the syllable *shin* meaning 'true'. It has Shinran (1173-1263) as its founder, but while he was alive there was no clear break with Jodoshu. With time there were two main differences, however: Jodoshu attaches great importance to the repetition of *nembutsu*, whereas Shin Buddhism gives faith the pride of place; and Jodoshu does not reject good acts as a means of salvation as markedly as Shin Buddhism.

Descent of Amida across the Mountains (Dahlem, Berlin)

In Shin Buddhist 'by faith alone' teaching there are many parallels to Lutheran Protestantism. It is said that the first Catholic missionaries had no success converting Shin Buddhists to Christianity, but wrote to the Pope that Lutherans had evidently come to Japan before them.

Shin Buddhism did not become a broad, popular religion until the time of Rennyo (1415-1499), the eighth descendant of Shinran. But over time it became so strong that in 1602 the Shogun, Tokugawa Ieyasu, in a clever move, divided the main temple in Kyoto into two: Nishi Honganji, 'The Western Temple of the Original Vow', and Higashi Honganji, 'The Eastern Temple of the Original Vow'.

There are 10 sub-sects of Shin Buddhism, but the remaining eight are small in comparison with Nishi Honganji, the oldest, and Higashi Honganji. The latter is also called *Shinshu Otani-ha* after the Otani family, who are direct descendants of Shinran. Also Nishi Honganji traces the highest priest and his family as such back to Shinran, and the hereditary priesthood is a strong tradition in Shin Buddhism as such.

Together, Jodoshu and Shin Buddhism have about 20 million followers in Japan today.

The sourcing of this book is mainly based on material from Higashi Honganji which, according to statistics, has 5.5 million members.

THE TEACHING OF SHIN BUDDHISM

The distinctive feature of Shin Buddhism is the concept of faith (*shinjin*), which is to be understood not as the result of one's own power (*jiriki*), but as a gift from the other power (*tariki*), i.e. Amida Buddha's gift to mankind achieved through his works of supererogation or merits. As long as people say 'I think' or 'I meditate' they are stuck with a false ego-consciousness, one of the cardinal sins of Buddhism as such. Shin Buddhists believe that Zen and esoteric Buddhism both rely on a false notion of self-power (*jiriki*).

In contrast to Jodoshu, the important moment is not salvation at the moment of death, but a 'moment of faith', the attainment of *shinjin*, in this life, something comparable to a conversion, but a conversion which is not due to the individual and which cannot be paraded,

Schematically, the teaching of Shin Buddhism can be set out as follows:

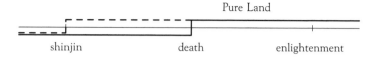

Pure Land

shinjin   death   enlightenment

It is to be noticed that birth in the Pure Land guarantees enlightenment later, but is not in itself enlightenment. To this comes the concept of *genzo* ('to return' in order to help more people to the Pure Land) which is a possibility after death and which is a clear influence of the bodhisattva ideal.

This can be compared with the following scheme from Chinese Amida Buddhism:

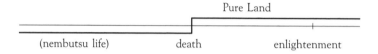

Pure Land

(nembutsu life)   death   enlightenment

As *shinjin* does not depend on good works it follows that Shin Buddhism as such has no strict set of morals. Morality flows from the gratitude of those assured of salvation. However, fairly early on there was a fusion of Confucian values with those of Shin Buddhism, as is the case in other types of Japanese Buddhism. And later Rennyo made rules for the conduct of the believers.

Among his followers Shinran is worshipped as an ideal person who dared to break with the existing schools of Buddhism, confident of Amida Buddha's salvation.

Another ideal can be found in the so-called *myokonin*, 'wondrous, happy people', who are uneducated, simple people who almost ecstatically devote themselves to Amida Buddha's care. What is intellectual belongs to Zen, whereas Shin cultivates the heart, Shin Buddhists claim. In spite of this claim Shin Buddhist thought is demanding and there is also a modern tradition of philosophical thinkers in Shin Buddhism which influenced the Kyoto School of Philosophers.

Another trait is the erasing of all distinctions among people due to Amida's all-embracing grace. Since there must be no separation between religion and ordinary life, even the principle of celibacy is rejected. Like their founder, Shinran, who described himself as 'neither priest nor layman', Shin priests are allowed to marry – and prefer marriage to celibacy. (In this matter Shin Buddhism has set the pattern for all other Buddhist sects in Japan.)

1 Shinran – the Founder

For believers there is no doubt about the high status of the founder. He is Shinran Shonin. The title, *shonin*, means 'eminent priest' – or 'saint' if translated into a similar category in Christianity. The Emperor Meiji bestowed on him the honourable name *Kenshin Daishi*, 'Great Teacher who has revealed the Truth'. This was a common practice among Japanese Emperors to give posthumous names to great teachers, signalling the social acceptance of the teaching. His importance is also seen in the size of his hall. In both Nishi and Higashi Honganji the Founder's Hall is bigger than even Amida's Hall. (See plan on p.104.)

Often in introductions to Shinran's life a four-part division is used:

- apprenticeship
- break with established Buddhism
- life in exile
- return to Kyoto as an accepted renewer of Buddhism

Shinran (1173-1263) belongs to the Kamakura period (1185-1333), when the military leaders, the Shoguns, had taken over from the Emperor. His family held high positions at the imperial court in Kyoto, but because of times of unrest many people at court sought a career as a Buddhist scholar monk. This was the case with Shinran who was educated as a monk on Mount Hiei outside Kyoto, thus starting his life with the prospect of following a traditional career in the Tendai sect, the most prominent at the time.

Instead, he chose his own path because of what to him were shortcomings in established Buddhism. In those days there was a general sense of decline of the spiritual meaning of Buddhism.

What exactly caused the break is unclear, but it was probably due to his spiritual despair at not being able to attain enlightenment by means of the rigorous disciplines prescribed by Tendai. However, Pure Land Buddhism was one of several accepted movements within Tendai, so Shinran's dissatisfaction must have been great. It was his own inability and anxiety for his future that made him leave Mount Hiei.

The next phase of his life found Honen (1133-1212) as the central character, the Pure Land master who had left Tendai Buddhism in 1175 and came to be the founder of Jodoshu. Shinran studied with Honen for six years, and during this time he also had an important revelation in a dream in the Rokkakudo temple in Kyoto where he undertook a one-hundred-day seclusion. During this time Shinran had a vision of Kannon Bosatsu, the bodhisattva of infinite compassion and the major attendant of Amida Buddha. (In Japan Prince Shotoku, 574-621, one of the most important persons in Japanese Buddhism, is considered a manifestation of Kannon, which is why Prince Shotoku has a prominent place in Shin Buddhism.)

The vision directed Shinran to Honen, and among other things he was perhaps also given permission to marry. This was a further incentive to break with the life of a monk. The second phase in Kyoto ends with the *nembutsu*-ban (1207), the prohibition against spreading the new teachings of Honen and Shinran. The Buddhist establishment of the time succeeded in persuading Japan's military rulers to impose the prohibition, and so Honen, Shinran and others had to go into exile in various parts of the country.

The third period was Shinran's exile in Echigo (today's Niigata) and Inada (today's Kanto area north of Tokyo). It was in this period that he married Eshinni from whom we have important letters. Here his awareness of the human condition deepened and his own interpretation of Buddhism matured. When the ban was lifted after five years in Echigo he chose not to go back to the centre of culture, Kyoto, but left for Inada, another desolate area.

A number of congregations were formed and it was during this period that Shinran became known for his most important work, *Kyogyoshinsho* (1224), which consists of commentaries to and excerpts from a selection of sutras in the Pure Land tradition. Modern scholarship, however, suggests that he never completed *Kyogyoshinsho*, but constantly revised the text. It was not until he was more than 60 years of age that he left the Kanto area to end his life in Kyoto.

In the fourth period, back in Kyoto, Shinran devoted his life to his writings and the dialogue with his disciples. Shinran wrote mainly in the native Japanese, and among other writings from this period, volumes of Japanese hymns (*wazan*) were very significant from the popular perspective. The *wazan* summarized his teaching and could be sung by his followers. The latter also turned to him for help in questions about the teachings; more than 50 letters from him to congregations in the Kanto area exist. His wife, Eshinni, lived in Echigo, but there are no signs of any estrangement. But between Shinran and his eldest son, Zenran, a conflict broke out when Zenran claimed direct authority from Shinran in his dealings with congregations in the Kanto region. In the end, Shinran had to disown him. In his last years Shinran was tended by his youngest daughter, Kakushinni, who was present at his death and arranged his burial. The chapel built at his tomb became the first Honganji, 'The temple of the original vow'.

MAP SHOWING SHINRAN'S ROUTE

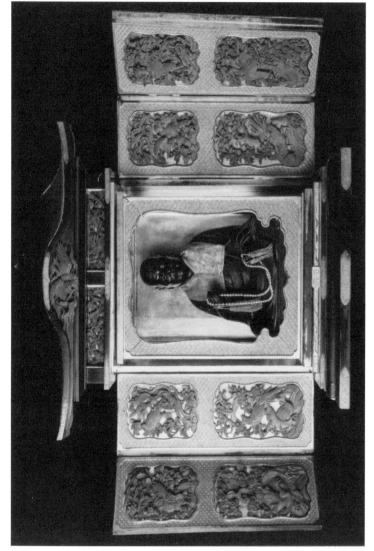

Shinran Shonin altar (Musée Guimet, Paris)

CHRONOLOGY OF SHINRAN'S LIFE:

1170
  Born at Hino, southeast of Kyoto (1173)
  Honen leaves Mt Hiei, founds Jodoshu (1175)
1180
  Shinran begins life as a monk on Mt Hiei, aged 9 (1181)
  Kamakura period begins (1185)
1190

1200
  Shinran leaves Mt Hiei, becomes Honen's disciple (1201)
  The *nembutsu* ban and beginning of exile in Echigo (1207)
1210 Marries Eshinni
  Pardoned (1211). Honen dies in Kyoto (1212)
  Shinran leaves for the Kanto area
1220
  Kyogyoshinsho (1224)

1230
  Return to Kyoto (1234)

1240

  First *wazan* in Japanese (1248)
1250
  Letters from congregations in Kanto (from 1251)
  Disowns his son, Zenran (1256)
1260
  Death in Kyoto (1263)

1270

Text 1

Eshinni: *Letter to Kakushinni*

*T*he letters of Shinran's wife, Eshinni, were not discovered until 1921, but are now considered the most reliable historical references to Shinran's life. The ten letters cover details of Eshinni's life and family matters. They do not contradict other sources, such as his biography called Godensho, by the great-grandson of Shinran, Kakunyo. [See Text 2.]

Of importance in this excerpt of a letter is the documentation that Shinran was a doso, a temple priest of Mount Hiei, and that he had a vision at the Rokkakudo temple in Kyoto which led him to Honen. Moreover, from the fact that Eshinni assures her daughter, Kakushinni, of Shinran's stature after his death, we may take it that Shinran's final moments were ordinary, in contrast to other founders of Buddhist religions whose deaths reputedly were accompanied by supernatural events.

I received your letter dated the 1st day of the 12th month of last year shortly after the 20th of the same month. There is no doubt that your father was reborn in the Pure Land, and there is no need for me to reiterate this.

The circumstances which led Shinran Shonin to confine himself to the Rokkakudo, chime with the words of Prince Shotoku in a dream, and brought him to the doors of Honen Shonin are next recorded.

He left Mt Hiei, remained in retreat for a hundred days at Rokkakudo, and prayed for salvation. Then, on the dawn of the ninety-fifth day, Prince Shotoku appeared in a dream, indicating the path to enlightenment by revealing a verse. He immediately left Rokkakudo in the morning, and he called on Master Honen to be shown the way of salvation. And just as he had confined himself for a hundred days at Rokkakudo, he visited Honen daily for a hundred days, rain or shine, regardless of the obstacles. He heard the Master teach that in order to be saved in the afterlife, regardless of whether one were good or evil, only the recitation of the Nembutsu was necessary. Since he carefully kept this teaching in his heart, he would say the following when people talked about the Nembutsu: 'Wherever Honen goes, I shall follow him, no matter what others may say – even if they say that I would go to hell, because I have wandered since the beginningless beginning and I have nothing to lose.'

□

This letter is to certify that your father was a *doso* at Mt Hiei, that he left the mountain and confined himself to the Rokkakudo for one hundred days, and that Prince Shotoku appeared and showed him the way, while praying for the salvation of all beings, in the dawn of the 95th day. In order that you can read it for yourself, I have written this and am sending it to you.

Lady Yoshiko Ohtani:
Eshin-ni – The Wife of Shinran Shonin
(Honpa Honganji. Kyoto, 1969-70)
pp. 31-32, 34

Text 2

Kakunyo: *Godensho*

*A*bout 34 years after his death, Shinran's great-grandson, Kakunyo, wrote a biography of Shinran which has ever since been revered by Shin Buddhists. The biography was from the beginning accompanied by pictures to dramatize the life of Shinran for unlettered people.

At the annual memorial rituals, called Ho-onko [see Text 30], one of the high points is the recitation of Godensho. To mark the occasion illustrations from Godensho are set up in all Shin Buddhist temples, and the believers often buy editions of Godensho in modern Japanese to be able to follow the highly stylized recitations. The following illustrations and edited commentaries are from such a popular edition found at Higashi Honganji, Kyoto. The order of the illustrations is the reverse of what is the norm in the West.

20

19

18

17

16

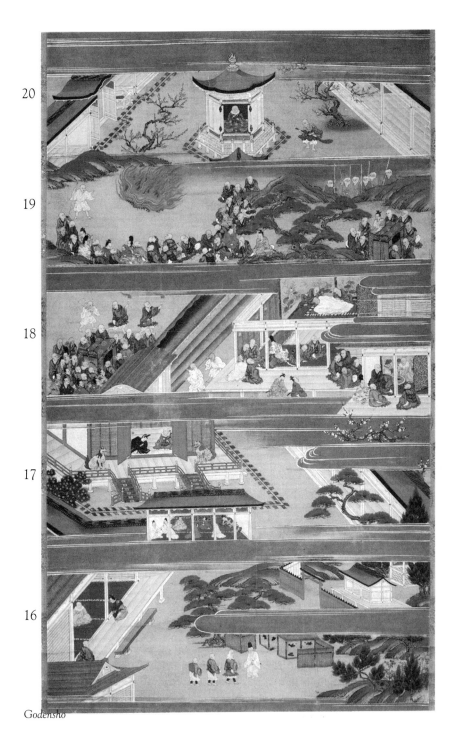

Godensho

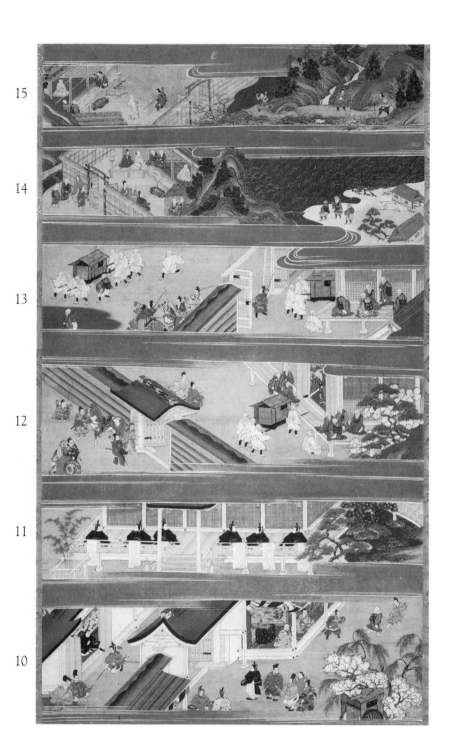

9

8

7

6

GODENSHO – EXPLANATION OF ILLUSTRATION

1. IN FRONT OF THE GATE OF SHOREN-IN.
Arrival at Shoren-in in an ox-carriage and registration as a monk.

2. IN SHOREN-IN'S GUESTROOM
In the presence of attendants and Shinran's uncle, Lord Noritsuna, Shinran's head is shaved; he becomes a monk (*tokudo*) and is taught dharma by Sojo Jien, a chief priest in Tendai Buddhism, in a scarlet robe.

3. ENTERING YOSHIMIZU TEMPLE.
Shinran in white (the picture has two stages) visits Honen at Yoshimizu where he is taught Pure Land Buddhism.

4. THE ORACLE AT ROKKAKU-DO.
Shinran (in grey) prays in front of Kannon in Rokkakudo. He is permitted to marry.

5. RENNI'S DREAM.
Renni, one of the first followers, in a dream sees Shotoku Taishi prostrating himself in front of Shinran (standing). In the dream Shotoku Taishi sees Shinran as an incarnation of Amida.

6. SHINRAN IS ENTRUSTED WITH THE SENJAKU-SHU BY HONEN
Shinran is allowed to copy Honen's Senjaku-shu, his principal work, and to copy his portrait, which Honen afterwards signs.

7. FAITH OR WORK
A discussion on whether faith (*shinjin*) or good work (*gyo*) lead to salvation. Shinran and Honen are in the minority group.

8. DISCUSSION OF SHINRAN'S FAITH
Shinran's statement that his faith (shinjin) and that of Honen is the same is doubted by the other priests, but Honen (centre) agrees with Shinran.

9. NYUSAIBO'S WISH AND JOZEN'S DREAM
Shinran reads his disciple Nyusaibo's wish and allows him to ask the painter Jozen to paint a picture of Shinran. Jozen is astonished to find that Shinran is almost identical in appearance with the Amida Buddha of the Zenko-ji temple, whom he had seen in a dream the night before.

10. THE PROHIBITION OF NEMBUTSU
Various officials from court and the authorities interrupt the Nembutsu teachings.

11. COURT NOBLES' DISCUSSION
The chief prosecutors discuss the prohibition of Nembutsu teaching.

12. THE BANISHMENT OF HONEN

13. THE BANISHMENT OF SHINRAN

14. ECHIGO PILGRIMS AND LATER DHARMA TEACHING IN INADA (HITACHI).
Shinran arrives at the Sea of Japan in Echigo (right) and later he starts preaching at Inada, Kanto (left).

15. THE CONVERSION AT ITAJIKI AND THE SALVATION OF BEN'EN.
Ben'en and other men of violence lie in wait for Shinran at Itajiki, Hitachi, but (in the next picture) Ben'en becomes a follower of Shinran, and throws away his sword and bow and arrows.

16. SHINRAN AT HAKONE AND BACK IN KYOTO
Shinran, at the mountain pass of Hakone on his way back to Kyoto, is greeted by an elderly man, a Shinto priest, who has been sent out to welcome Shinran by the Shinto god, Gongen.

17. KUMANO SHRINE
Heitaro, a disciple, in a dream sees the Shinto priest of Kumano bow to Shinran.

18. SHINRAN EXPLAINS DHARMA ON HIS SICK-BED, DIES IN KYOTO AND IS TAKEN TO HIS FUNERAL

19. THE CREMATION OF SHINRAN.
The scene has two stages: Shinran in the coffin and Shinran in the cremation fire.

20. SHINRAN'S ORIGINAL MAUSOLEUM IS ESTABLISHED
The *hombyo* (original mausoleum) was built by Shinran's daughter, Kakushinni, 15 years after his death.

Text 3

Shinran: *Tannisho [chapters 1, 3 and 15]*

*T*annisho *is a collection of quotations by Shinran put down and commented on by the disciple Yuien in the thirteenth century. The meaning of the title is 'A record of the words of Shinran set down in lamentation over departures from his teaching'. The title indicates the crisis confronting Shinran's followers at the time with respect to the meaning and implications of his teachings. Yuien refutes many misunderstandings, while attempting to maintain the spirit of Shinran.*

For centuries afterwards the book itself was largely unknown, even to Shin Buddhists, and in a manuscript version that belonged to Rennyo (1415-99), the important organizer of Shin Buddhism in the fifteenth century, Rennyo himself wrote: 'This writing is an important one in our tradition. It should not be indiscriminately shown to anyone who lacks the past karmic good.'

It was popularized by the Shin reformer, Kiyozawa Manshi (1863-1903), see Text 6, and today it is one of the most widely read of Japanese Buddhist classics.

■ 1

'Saved by the inconceivable working of Amida's Vow. I shall realize birth into the Pure Land': the moment you entrust yourself thus, so that the mind set upon saying the Name arises within you, you are brought to share in the benefit of being grasped by Amida, never to be abandoned.

Know that the Primal Vow of Amida makes no distinction between people young and old, good and evil: only the entrusting of yourself to it is essential. For it was made to save the person in whom karmic evil is deep-rooted and whose blind passions abound.

Thus, entrusting yourself to the Primal Vow requires no performance of good, for no act can hold greater virtue than saying the Name. Nor is there need to despair of the evil you commit, for no act is so evil that it obstructs the working of Amida's Primal Vow.

Thus were his words.

□

■ 3

Even a good person can attain birth in the Pure Land, so it goes without saying that an evil person will.

Though such is the truth, people commonly say, 'Even an evil person attains birth, so naturally a good person will.' This statement may seem well-founded at first, but it runs counter to the meaning of Other Power established through the Primal Vow. For a person who relies on the good that he does through his self-power fails to entrust himself wholeheartedly to Other Power and therefore is not in accord with Amida's Primal Vow.

But when he abandons his attachment to self-power and entrusts himself totally to Other Power, he will realize birth in the Pure Land.

It is impossible for us, filled as we are with blind passions, to free ourselves from birth-and-death through any practice whatever. Sorrowing at this, Amida made the Vow, the essential intent of which is the attainment of Buddhahood by the person who is evil. Hence the evil person who entrusts himself to Other Power is precisely the one who possesses the true cause for birth.

Accordingly, he said: 'Even the virtuous man is born in the Pure Land, so without question is the man who is evil.'

□

■ 15

Concerning the assertion that one attains enlightenment even while maintaining this bodily existence full of blind passions:
This statement is completely absurd.

The attainment of Buddhahood with this very body is the fundamental intent of Shingon esotericism; it is the realization achieved through the three kinds of mystic acts. The enlightenment known as the purification of the six sense organs is the One Vehicle teaching of the Lotus Sutra; it is the virtue attained through the four practices of repose. These are ways of difficult practice to be followed by those of superior capacity, of the enlightenment realized through contemplative practice. The unfolding of enlightenment in the coming life is the essence of the Pure Land teaching of Other Power: it is the reality at work in the settlement of shinjin. This is the way of easy practice to be followed by those of inferior capacity, of the dharma that does not differentiate between the good and the evil.

Since it is extremely difficult to free oneself from blind passions and the hindrances of karmic evil, even the virtuous monks who practise the Shingon and the Tendai teachings aspire after all for enlightenment in the next life. What more need be said? We lack both observance of precepts and wisdom, but when, by allowing ourselves to be carried on the ship of Amida's Vow, we have crossed this ocean of birth-and-death, so full of suffering, and attained the shore of the Pure Land, then the moon of awakening to things as they truly are will immediately appear, and becoming one with the unhindered light filling the ten quarters, we will benefit all sentient beings. At that moment we attain enlightenment.

Do those who speak of realizing enlightenment while in this bodily existence manifest, as the revered Śākyamuni did, various accommodated bodies to guide beings to enlightenment in accordance with their capacities; do they possess the Buddha's thirty-two marks and eighty secondary good features, and preach the dharma and benefit beings? This is the paradigm of realizing enlightenment in this life.

Shinran states in a hymn:

> Looking to and encountering the moment
> When *shinjin*, firm and diamondlike,
>   becomes settled:
> In that instant Amida's compassionate light
>   grasps and protects us,
> So that we part forever from birth-and-death.

At the moment *shinjin* becomes settled, a person is immediately grasped, never to be abandoned, and therefore he will not transmigrate further in the six paths; thus, 'We part forever from birth-and-death'. Should realizing this be confusedly labelled 'enlightenment'? Such misunderstanding is indeed pitiful.

The late master said:

> According to the true essence of the Pure Land way, one entrusts oneself to the Primal Vow in this life and realizes enlightenment in the Pure Land; this is the teaching I received.

> (*Tannishō: A Primer* (Ryukoku University, Kyoto, 1991), p. 22, 23-24, 37-39)

Text 4

Shinran: *Mattosho* [excerpts from letters 1, 2 and 20]

Shinran's letters are mostly from the last period in his life, from 1251-62, when Shinran was between 79 and 90 years old and lived in Kyoto. Altogether, there are more than 40 letters and 22 are to be found in Mattosho, 'Lamp for the Latter Age'. They were answers to enquiries made by congregations about various doctrinal matters, and Shinran's responses, of which copies were preserved, were highly valued by the individual congregations. Even though the contents often involve difficult controversial questions, Shinran as a person also emerges clearly in the letters.

■ 1

The idea of Amida's coming at the moment of death is for those who seek to gain birth in the Buddha Land by doing religious practices, for they are practicers of self-power. The moment of death is of central concern for such people, for they have not yet attained true *shinjin*. We may also speak of Amida's coming at the moment of death in the case of the person who, though he has committed the ten transgressions and the five grave offences throughout his life, encounters a teacher in the hour of death and is led at the very end to utter the *nembutsu*.

The person who lives true shinjin, however, abides in the stage of the truly settled, for he has already been grasped, never to be abandoned. There is no need to wait in anticipation for the moment of death, no need to rely on Amida's coming. At the time shinjin becomes settled, birth, too, becomes settled; there is no need for the deathbed rites that prepare one for Amida's coming.

□

■ 2

According to Shin Buddhism, there are two kinds of people who seek birth in the Buddha Land: those of Other Power and those of self-power. This has been taught by the Indian masters and Jōdo patriarchs. Self-power is the effort to attain birth, whether by invoking the names of Buddhas other than Amida and practising good acts other than the nembutsu, in accordance with your particular circumstances and opportunities, or by endeavouring to make yourself worthy through amending the confusion in your acts, words and thoughts, confident of your own powers and guided by your own calculation. Other Power is the entrusting of yourself to the 18th among Amida Tathagata's Vows, the Primal Vow of birth through nembutsu, which Amida selected from among all other practices. Since this is the Vow of Tathagata, Hōnen said: 'In Other Power, no self-working is true working.' 'Self-working' is a term which connotes calculation. Since the calculation of the person seeking birth is self-power, it is self-working. Other Power is entrusting ourselves to the Primal Vow and our birth becoming firmly settled; hence it is altogether without self-working. Thus, on the one hand, you should not be anxious that Tathagata will not receive you because you do wrong. A foolish being is by nature possessed of blind passion, so you must recognize yourself as being a karmic evil. On the other hand, you should not think that you deserve to attain birth because you are good. You cannot be born into the true and real Buddha Land through such self-power calculation. I have been taught that with a shinjin of self-power a person can attain birth only in the land of indolence, the borderland, the womb of the Buddha Land, or the castle of doubt.

Through the fulfilment of the 18th Primal Vow, Bodhisattva Dharmakara has become Amida Tathagata, and the benefit that surpasses conceptual understanding has come to transcend all bounds; to express this, Bodhisattva Vasubandhu uses the words, 'the Tathagata of unhindered light filling the ten quarters'. Truly know, therefore, that without any differentiation between good and bad people, and regardless of one's having a heart of blind passion, all beings are certain to attain birth. Describing the manner of entrusting in the nembutsu of the Primal Vow, Genshin, Master of Eshin-in, states in his *Essentials for Attaining Birth*: 'It makes no difference whether you are walking, standing still, sitting, or lying, nor is there choice to be made among times, places, or other circumstances.' He affirms beyond question that the person who has attained true shinjin has been grasped by the compassionate light. And so, as Sakyamuni has taught, at the very moment that we, possessed of ignorance and blind passion, are born into the Buddha Land of Peace, we attain the supreme Buddhahood.

□

■ 20

There was a time for each of you when you knew nothing of Amida's Vow and did not say the name of Amida Buddha, but now, guided by the compassionate means of Sakyamuni and Amida, you have begun to hear the Vow. Formerly, you were drunk with the wine of ignorance and had a taste only for the three poisons of greed, anger, and folly, but since you have begun to hear the Buddha's Vow you have gradually awakened from the drunkenness of ignorance, gradually rejected the three poisons, and come to prefer at all times the medicine of Amida Buddha.

In contrast, how lamentable that people who have not fully awakened from drunkenness are urged to more drunkenness and those still in the grip of poison encouraged to take yet more poison. It is indeed sorrowful to give way to impulses with the excuse that one is by nature possessed of blind passion – excusing acts that should not be committed, words that should not be said, and thoughts that should not be harboured – and to say that one may follow one's desires in any way whatever. It is like offering more wine before the person has become sober or urging him to take even more poison before the poison has abated. 'Here's some medicine, so drink all the poison you like' – words like these should never be said.

In people who have long heard the Buddha's Name and said the nembutsu, surely there are signs of rejecting the evil of this world and signs of their desire to cast off the evil in themselves. When people first begin to hear the Buddha's Vow, they wonder, having become thoroughly aware of the karmic evil in their hearts and minds, how they will ever attain birth as they are. To such people we teach that since we are possessed of blind passion, the Buddha receives us without judging whether our hearts are good or bad.

When, upon hearing this, a person's trust in the Buddha has grown deep, he comes to abhor such a self and to lament his continued existence in birth-and-death; and he then joyfully says the Name of Amida Buddha, deeply entrusting himself to the Vow. That he seeks to stop doing wrong as his heart moves him, although earlier he gave thought to such things and committed them as his mind dictated, is surely a sign of his having rejected this world.

Moreover, since shinjin which aspires for the attainment of birth arises through the encouragement of Sakyamuni and Amida, once the true and real mind is made to arise in us, how can we remain as we were, possessed of blind passion? There are reports of some wrongdoing even of some among you. I have heard of their slandering the master, holding their true teachers in contempt and belittling their fellow practitioners – all of which is deeply saddening. They are already guilty of slandering the dharma and committing the five grave offences. Do not associate with them. The *Treatise on the Buddha Land* states that such thoughts arise because they fail to entrust themselves to the Buddha dharma. Moreover, in explaining the mind of sincerity it teaches that one should keep a respectful distance and not become familiar with those who give themselves to such wrongdoing. It teaches us rather to draw close to and become friends with our teachers and fellow-practicers. As for becoming friends with those who are given to wrongdoing, it is only after we go to the Buddha Land and return to benefit sentient beings that we can become close to and friendly with them. That, however, is not our own design; only by being saved by Amida's Vow can we act as we want. But at this moment, as we are, what can we possibly do? Please consider this very carefully. Since the diamond-like heart that aspires for birth is awakened through the Buddha's working, the person who realizes the diamond-like heart will surely not slander his master or be contemptuous of his true teachers.

Mattōshō
(Letters of Shinran (Shin Buddhism
Translation Series, Honganji
International Center, 1978),
p. 19-20, 22-24, 60-62)

Text 5

Shinran: *Shoshinge – Hymn of True Shinjin and Nembutsu*

Shoshinge has been called 'the heart of Shin Buddhism' and it is impossible to participate in ceremonies in Shin temples without realizing its great popularity. It is by far the best known of Shinran's hymns and the one his followers sing loudest. It it sold from the main temples on cassette tapes sung by large choirs. In brief, it contains a summary account of the Pure Land lineage and the theological basis of

Shin Buddhism.

In Shinran's works it is included in *Kyogyoshinsho* (*(Collection of passages on) Teaching, Practice, Faith and Realization*), his main doctrinal work, which is a systematic collection of Pure Land texts, commented on and interpreted by Shinran.

SHOSHINGE – HYMN OF TRUE SHINJIN AND THE NEMBUTSU

I take refuge in the Tathagata of Immeasurable Life!
I entrust myself to the Buddha of Inconceivable Light!
Bodhisattva Dharmākara, in his causal stage,
Under the guidance of Lokeśvararāja Buddha,

Searched into the origins of the Buddha's pure lands,
And the qualities of those lands and their men and devas;
He then established the supreme, incomparable Vow;
He made the great Vow rare and all-encompassing.

In five kalpas of profound thought, he embraced this Vow,
Then resolved again that his Name be heard throughout ten
    quarters.
Everywhere he casts light immeasurable, boundless,
Unhindered, unequalled, light-lord of all brilliance,

Pure light, joyful light, the light of wisdom,
Light constant, inconceivable, light beyond speaking,
Light excelling sun and moon he sends forth, illumining countless
    worlds;
The multitudes of beings all receive the radiance.

The Name embodying the Primal Vow is the act of true
    settlement,
The Vow of entrusting with sincere mind is the cause of birth;
We realize the equal of enlightenment and supreme nirvana
Through the fulfilment of the Vow attaining nirvana without
    fail.

Sākyamuni Tathagata appeared in this world
Solely to teach the ocean-like Primal Vow of Amida;

We, an ocean of beings in an evil age of five defilements,
Should entrust ourselves to Tathagata's words of truth.

When the one thought-moment of joy arises,
Nirvana is attained without severing blind passions;
When ignorant and wise, even grave offenders and slanders of the
    dharma, all alike turn and enter shinjin,
They are like waters that, on entering the ocean, become one in
    taste with it.

The light of compassion that grasps us illumines and protects us
    always;
The darkness of our ignorance is already broken through;
Still the clouds and mists of greed and desire, anger and hatred,
Cover as always the sky of true and real shinjin.

But though light of the sun is veiled by clouds and mists,
Beneath the clouds and mists there is brightness, not dark.
When one realizes shinjin, seeing and revering and attaining great
    joy,
One immediately leaps crosswise, closing off the five evil courses.

All foolish beings, whether good or evil,
When they hear and entrust to Amida's universal Vow,
Are praised by the Buddha as people of vast and excellent
    understanding;
Such a person is called a pure white lotus.

For evil sentient beings of wrong views and arrogance,
The nembutsu that embodies Amida's Primal Vow
Is hard to accept in shinjin;
This most difficult of difficulties, nothing surpasses.

The masters of India in the west, who explained the teaching in
    treatises,
And the eminent monks of China and Japan,
Clarified the Great Sage's true intent in appearing in the world,
And revealed that Amida's Primal Vow accords with the nature of
    beings.

Śākyamuni Tathagata, on Mount Laṅkā,
Prophesied to the multitudes that in south India

The mahasattva Nāgārjuna would appear in this world
To crush the views of being and non-being.

Proclaiming the unexcelled Mahayana teaching,
He would attain the stage of joy and be born in the land of
   happiness.
Nāgārjuna clarifies the hardship on the overland path of difficult
   practice,
And lead us to entrust the pleasure on the waterway of easy
   practice.

He teaches that the moment one thinks on Amida's Primal Vow,
One is naturally brought to enter the stage of the definitely settled;
Solely saying the Tathagata's Name constantly,
One should respond with gratitude to the universal Vow of great
   compassion.

Bodhisattva Vasubandhu, composing a treatise, declares
That he takes refuge in the Tathagata of unhindered light,
And that relying on the sutras, he will reveal the true and real
   virtues,
And making widely known the great Vow by which we leap
   crosswise beyond birth-and-death.

He discloses the mind that is single so that all beings be saved
By Amida's directing of virtue through the power of the Primal
   Vow.
When a person turns and enters the great treasure-ocean of virtue,
Necessarily he joins Amida's assembly.

And when he reaches that lotus-held world,
He immediately realizes the body of suchness or dharma-nature.
Then sporting in the forests of blind passions, he manifests
   transcendent powers;
Entering the garden of birth-and-death, he assumes various forms
   to guide others.

Turning towards the dwelling of Master Tanluan, the Emperor of
   Liang
Always paid homage to him as a bodhisattva.
Bodhiruci, master of the Tripitaka, gave Tanluan the Pure Land
   teachings,

And Tanluan, burning his Taoist scriptures, took refuge in the
land of bliss.

In his commentary on the treatise of Bodhisattva Vasubandhu,
He shows that the cause and attainment of birth in the fulfilled
land lie in the Vow.
Our going and returning, directed to us by Amida, come about
through Other Power;
The truly decisive cause is shinjin.

When a foolish being of delusion and defilement awakens shinjin,
He realizes that birth-and-death is itself nirvana;
Without fail he reaches the land of immeasurable light
And universally guides sentient beings to enlightenment.

Daochuo determined how difficult it is to fulfill the Path of Sages,
And reveals that only passage through the Pure Land gate is
possible for us.
He criticizes self-power endeavour in the myriad good practices,
And encourages us solely to say the fulfilled Name embodying true
virtue.

With kind concern he teaches the three characteristics of
entrusting and non-entrusting,
Compassionately guiding all identically, whether they live when
the dharma survives as but form, when in its last stage, or when
it has become extinct.
Though a person has committed evil all his life, when he
encounters the Primal Vow,
He will reach the world of peace and realize the perfect fruit of
enlightenment.

Shandao alone in his time clarified the Buddha's true intent;
Sorrowing at the plight of meditative and non-meditative
practicers and people of grave evil,
He reveals that Amida's light and Name are the causes of birth.
When the practicer enters the great ocean of wisdom, the Primal
Vow,

He receives the diamond-like mind
And accords with the one thought-moment of joy; whereupon,
Equally with Vaidehī, he acquires the threefold wisdom

And is immediately brought to attain the eternal bliss of dharma-
nature.

Genshin, having broadly elucidated the teachings of Śākyamuni's
lifetime,
Wholeheartedly took refuge in the land of peace and urges all to do
so;
Ascertaining that minds devoted to single practice are profound,
to sundry practice, shallow,
He sets forth truly the difference between the fulfilled land and the
transformed land.

The person burdened with extreme evil should simply say the
Name:
Although I too am within Amida's grasp,
Passions obstruct my eyes and I cannot see him;
Nevertheless, great compassion is untiring and illumines me
always.

Master Genkū [Honen], well-versed in the Buddha's teaching,
Turned compassionately to foolish people, both good and evil;
Establishing in this remote land the teaching and realization that
are the true essence of the Pure Land way,
He transmits the selected Primal Vow to us of the defiled world:

Return to this house of transmigration, of birth-and-death,
Is decidedly caused by doubt.
Swift entrance into the city of tranquillity, the uncreated,
Is necessarily brought about by shinjin.

The mahasattvas and masters who spread the sutras
Save the countless beings of utter defilement and evil.
With the same mind, all people of the present, whether monk or
lay,
Should rely wholly on the teachings of these venerable masters.

Kyōgyōshinshō
(The True Teaching, Practice and
Realization of the Pure Land Way,
Chapter on Practice (Shin Buddhism
Translation Series, Honganji
International Center), Vol. I, p. 160-67.

2 Shin Buddhism in the Modern Age

Shinran never explicitly indicated any intention to found a new Buddhist movement, nor does he exhibit any consciousness other than that he was a follower of Honen. However, his writings and correspondence with his followers provided the foundations for a new movement. The process of institutionalization began with his daughter, Kakushinni (1224-82), who established his mausoleum as a place of pilgrimage for the disciples who lived far away from Kyoto. The third abbot, Kakunyo (1270-1351), transformed the mausoleum into a temple called Honganji. He strove to unify the Shin Buddhist movement under his leadership by claiming hereditary and spiritual lineage from Shinran. Nevertheless, despite his efforts, the Honganji had to compete with the more popular Bukkoji and Takada branches for adherents. From Kakunyo to Rennyo (1415-99), the eighth abbot, the fortunes of the Honganji languished.

Rennyo was a propagator with a stroing charismatic personality and a burning desire to revive the fortunes of the Honganji. He is, therefore, called the Restorer of the sect in contrast to Shinran who founded it. Through his endeavours, Honganji became a leading religious and social force with close involvement in the *Ikko Ikki* peasant uprisings. It drew the attention of Shoguns who aspired to unify the country and control the Buddhist sects, such as Nobunaga who struggled with Honganji for ten years before defeating it, and Hideyoshi who favoured Honganji in face of the growth of Christianity in the late sixteenth century. Finally, as we saw earlier, Tokugawa Ieyasu took the opportunity to divide the sect into Nishi (West) Honganji and Higashi (East) Honganji in

Kiyozawa Manshi Nanjo Bunyu Sasaki Gessho

D.T. Suzuki Soga Ryojin Kaneko Daiei Yamaguchi Susumu

Key people of Shin Buddhism in the modern age (Otani University)

order to undermine the sect's political power.

Today, the Tokugawa era is not highly regarded by Shin Buddhists for its spiritual development. The followers of the religion became pious and obedient, but at the same time the temples became very important to the shogunate to combat Christianity. The government required all Japanese citizens to register their families in Buddhist temples generally and organized the temples under head temples responsible to the government. The clergy became complacent. When the Meiji government abolished this system in 1868, Buddhism had a rude awakening with the loss of government support and popular reaction against Buddhism which led to the destruction of temples and many historical treasures. In addition, there was the reappearance of active Christian missions with the opening of Japan to the West.

These new conditions generated a response towards Buddhist reform in which Kiyozawa Manshi (1863-1903) played a major role. Of lower samurai background he became one of the great Meiji educators, and among his other achievements he reorganized the educational facility which is known today as Otani University. His main concern, however, was to cultivate a deeper spiritual life in Shin Buddhism. Indirectly he played a part in the World Parliament of Religions in Chicago 1893 where his *Skeleton of a Philosophy of Religion* was submitted for discussion.

Almost all modern thinkers in Shinshu Otani-ha (Higashi

Honganji) trace their disciple relationship to Kiyozawa Manshi. These include such notables as Akegarasu Haya (1877-1967), Maida Shuichi (1906-67), as well as Soga Ryojin (1875-1971) and Kaneko Daiei (1881-1976) who were prominent in doctrinal studies.

Daisetz T. Suzuki (1870-1966), who is well known in the West for his Zen studies, reflects another stream in modern Shin Buddhism, that of Buddhist scholarship. With a Zen father and a Shin Buddhist mother, his Zen training, his knowledge of English and his stay in the USA made him a perfect East-West 'bridge-builder'. His life-long contributions to *The Eastern Buddhist* on Shin Buddhism resulted in the posthumous *Collected Writings on Shin Buddhism* (1973), together with his almost completed translation of Shinran's major text *Kyogyoshinsho*.

(It should be noted in passing here that the selection of modern Shin Buddhist thinkers in this chapter is dominated by the Higashi Honganji school, because the research was carried out at Otani University.)

Text 6

Kiyozawa Manshi: *On Faith and Reason*

The reformer of Shin Buddhism, Kiyozawa Manshi (1863-1901), studied Western philosophy at Tokyo University under Ernest F. Fenollosa, among others, and one of his major works is 'A Skeleton of a Philosophy of Religion' (1892) from which the following excerpt is taken. In it he strangely echoes the contemporary debate on religion and science in the West.

3. *Faith and Reason.* It may be urged that, not the religious faculty or *faith* alone, but the intellectual faculty or *reason* also has the infinite for its object. Is not *philosophy* conversant about the infinite? Yes, indeed; but philosophy intends to *investigate* it while religion *believes* it. A few words for a further explanation. Reason or philosophy begins with the search about the infinite and never stops its pursuit until it finally grasps at it; when, however, it grasps at it or realizes its object, the work of reason is over, and philosophy is finished: And this is just the starting point of faith or religion. In other words, faith or religion begins by believing the

existence of the infinite and tries to enjoy its blessings. So we may state that, at the point where philosophy completes its work, there begins the business of religion. It is by no means thereby implied that, unless we finished the philosophical task, we should not be allowed to enter the gate of religion. I have been speaking only about the order in which the intellectual investigation and the religious belief should be arranged. But there is no need of studying philosophy for those who can at once believe in the existence of the infinite. Such being the case, we take up the old distinction and say that *philosophy accords to the demands of reason and religion to those of faith*.

4. *The Relation of Reason to Faith*. Does then the religion reject the use of reason within its province? By no means. Although its fundamental characteristic is belief, yet it never refuses the service of reason in explaining and extinguishing the *doubts* which arise in the bosom of religion itself. Nay, more; sometimes reason is indispensable to religion. When the wise or the learned endeavours to attain to religion, it is very proper for him to start or propose doubts about it and, then, upon the solution of those doubts, gladly embrace the doctrine. Here is a point requiring attention of our readers. We have asserted that religion depends on belief; *but we do not mean it requires unreasoned or unreasonable belief*. On the contrary, if there are two propositions, the one of reason and the other of faith, we should rather take the former instead of the latter. For we are sure that true propositions will be true both to reason and to faith, and that propositions of reason can be corrected by other propositions of reason while those of faith are devoid of such means of correction. But remember that *the nature of reason is incompleteness*, *i.e.* reason can never be complete in its range or series of propositions, one proposition linking to or depending on the other *ad infinitum*, so that if any one relies on reason alone, he might never be able to attain the solid resting place of religious belief. This characteristic incompleteness of reason may be a warning to the seekers of scientific truths. Why is A? Because of B. Why is B? Because of C. Why is C? Because of D. And so on without end. Such is the chain of proofs or grounds. Reason can never stop and rest. If it stops and rests at any point, it must be just a point of belief. Hence reason must ultimately rely on faith for its foundation. In cases, however, of many or conflicting propositions, those must be selected which harmonize with fundamental beliefs and those rejected which are in conflict with

them. Thus *selection and regulation* are the proper functions of reason, not only with regard to religious propositions, but also in all propositions of science and knowledge. Such being the case, we conclude that *Faith and Reason should always help, and can never conflict with, each other.*

The Skeleton of a Philosophy of Religion
(Tokyo 1893), p. 2-5

Text 7

Kiyozawa Manshi: *Peace Beyond Ethics*

*K*iyozawa Manshi, *although of lower samurai origin, did not submit to ordinary Confucian ethics. Among modern Shin Buddhist scholars he is compared to religious existentialists in Europe. Man must choose to rely on the Buddha.*

About his anti-authoritarian and independent attitude, see also the introduction to Text 38.

The famous Japanese general Taira no Shigemori (1138-79) is said to have been a man of great wisdom, but from a religious point of view that is not rue. I say this because as he prepared himself for death he said with a sigh of resignation, 'To be loyal to the emperor I must be unfilial to my parents. To be filial to my parents I must be disloyal to the emperor. I know not what I, Shigemori, must do.' From the standpoint of ethics, he might seem to be a man of great wisdom. But I find it pathetic that he fretted about such questions to an extent that they incapacitated him and drove him to his death. Shigemori, in short, had based his life merely on ethics. As a result, he could not help but suffer. We must have a spiritual basis that goes beyond ethics and that enables us to be calm in any given situation. We must arrive at the great spiritual peace that will enable us to live calmly in the present moment.

□

Let me clarify my point with an example from everyday life. Picture a little boy carrying food on a tray for a guest. His mother is worried that he might stumble, so she follows closely behind, supporting the tray. Although the boy is convinced that he is carrying the tray by himself, he happens to look back. He discovers that it is actually his mother that has been supporting the tray. When he is not aware of his mother's help and thinks that he is the only one carrying the tray, he is worried about dropping it. But when he discovers that his mother is helping, he can forget about his self and his responsibility, and leave everything to her.

The person who has awakened to the working of Tathāgata may sometimes revert to the realm of the self and, out of a sense of responsibility, may fall into suffering and distress. However, he can immediately return to reliance on Tathāgata and feel the burden of his responsibility lifted. Before, he felt cornered by responsibilities. Now, he can see the vast world opening up through Tathāgata. When we fall back into the realm of self, we are attacked by suffering and distress. But as soon as we return to reliance on Tathāgata, the self is nullified. Whatever we do or see is completely embraced by the warm, spring-like compassion of Tathāgata. Our suffering is transformed into gratitude. Even words such as 'tragic' or 'pathetic' are not sufficient to describe the person who has yet to awaken to this great peace beyond ethics. It is tragic that Shigemori, with his merely ethical way of thinking, died worrying about such trivial matters and that he was unable to enter the tremendous sphere of the wondrous working of Tathāgata.

For the person who has awakened to the wondrous working of Tathāgata, there is no such thing as being a failure in life. I say this because failure simply does not exist as an objective reality. It exists only when we in our minds regard ourselves as failures and become depressed. For a person who believes that all things are guided by the hands of Tathāgata, there may be things that encourage and instruct him, but nothing that would make him see himself as a failure. Socrates accepted his fate, drank the hemlock, and died. Shinran Shōnin courageously went into exile with a feeling of gratitude, believing that exile was a favour granted him by his master's teaching. Those individuals who were in the presence of the wondrous working did not see themselves as failures in any sense.

(1902)
(Published in *December Fan* (Higashi Honganji,
Kyoto, 1984), p. 37, 41-42)

Text 8

Kiyozawa Manshi:
My Religious Conviction

O*n 30 May 1903, one week before his death, Kiyozawa Manshi wrote his religious will whose original title by Kiyozawa was 'Thus I Trust in Tathagata'. Later, it became known as 'My Religious Conviction'.*

I have briefly answered the three questions that I posed in this essay. My first point – that trust in Tathāgata gives me the benefit of relief – means that Tathāgata is infinite compassion. The second point – that trust becomes a reality when my intellectual pursuit reaches its limit – means that Tathāgata is infinite wisdom. The third point – that trust in Tathāgata enables me to live – means that Tathāgata is infinite power.

First, since Tathāgata is infinite compassion, Tathāgata enables me to have peace and tranquillity as soon as my religious conviction is established. Without waiting until the world after death, the Tathāgata in which I trust has already given me the greatest happiness in this life. It is not that other things do not make me happy, too. They may give me some measure of happiness. But nothing else can give me such tremendous happiness as my religious conviction. So the happiness provided by religious conviction is the greatest happiness for me in this life. It is the happiness that I am actually experimenting with day in and day out. As far as happiness in the world after death is concerned, I can make no comment now, because I have not actually experimented with that.

Second, since Tathāgata is infinite wisdom, Tathāgata constantly protects me by enlightening me, by dispelling the darkness of my ignorance, and by delivering me from delusions and wrong views. By force of habit, I inadvertently get involved in futile efforts, such as scholarly investigation or examination. At times, I even set out to prove the reality of the Infinite on the basis of my finite and unsophisticated way of thinking. Even when I fall victim to that habit, I soon recognize its futility and abandon it, thanks to my religious conviction.

'Know that you do not know. That is Knowledge' (Socrates).

That is actually the apex of human knowledge, but it is not easily accepted by us. I used to have all kinds of presumptuous opinions. But now, thanks to my religious conviction, I am able to truly appreciate the humble names our teachers gave themselves, such as 'Hōnen the Foolish' (Guchi no Hōnen-bō), or 'Foolish Baldheaded Shinran' (Gutoku no Shinran). Now I can be content with the fact that I, too, am ignorant.

Although I was aware that the human intellect is finite and imperfect, I was unable to rid myself of the delusion that I could find an absolute basis for ethics and religion, or explain the reality of the Infinite by human intellect. I used to think that the world would collapse and society would fall into disorder if I did not have a criterion for judging truth. But now I am firmly convinced that I cannot possibly establish such a criterion on the basis of human intellect.

Third, since Tathāgata is infinite power, Tathāgata, through my religious conviction, endows me with a great ability to live. We normally rely upon common sense in determining what action should be taken. But that no longer works when things get complicated. Then people like myself start to think, ponder, and investigate in an attempt to discover some basis for ethics and religion. As a result, decisions about my own conduct become all the more difficult and I become utterly perplexed. We all know that we should not speak indiscreetly, we should not behave improperly, we should not break the law, we should not act immorally, we should not be impolite, we should not forget our manners. We also know that we must accept responsibility for ourselves, strangers, parents, husband, wife, children, sisters, brothers, friends, good people, bad people, the elderly, and the young. In this case, we are talking about only the most basic ethical principles and we find it difficult to fulfil even these. Anyone who has earnestly tried to observe each and every one of his ethical principles will have to admit that the task is impossible. I have suffered a great deal under that impossible burden. Had I no other prospect than to bear that impossible burden, I would have committed suicide long ago. But religion has relieved me of my suffering and I no longer feel any need to resort to suicide. That is to say, I now have peace and comfort through my trust in Tathāgata, the infinite compassion.

How does Tathāgata, the infinite compassion, enable me to attain such peace of mind? In no other way than by assuming the burden of my every responsibility. Nothing, not even the worst evil, can hinder the working of Tathāgata. There is no need for me to deliberate on what is good or evil, right or wrong. There is nothing I cannot do. I act as I please and I do as I am inclined. There is no need for me to be concerned about my every action, even if it turns out to be a mistake or a crime. Tathāgata takes on the burden of responsibility for all of my actions. I need only trust in Tathāgata to live in constant peace of mind.

The power of Tathāgata is limitless. The power of Tathāgata is unsurpassed. The power of Tathāgata is omnipresent. It pervades everything and works freely, without hindrance. By committing myself to the wondrous power of Tathāgata, I have great peace and comfort. By entrusting the great question of life and death to Tathāgata, I have no fear, no discontentment.

A passage says: 'Life and death, wealth and nobility are appointed by the Mandate of Heaven' (*Analects of Confucius*). The Tathāgata in which I trust is this Mandate of Heaven, the basic reality underlying our existence.

(1903)
(Published in *December Fan* (Higashi Honganji,
Kyoto, 1984), p. 57-60

Text 9

Akegarasu Haya: *About Wisdom*

A kegarasu Haya (1877-1967), born in a village Shinshu temple in northern Japan, was a disciple of Kiyozawa Manshi for ten years until Kiyozawa's death, and afterwards he spread modern Shinshu teachings during his many travels. He became head of the Higashi Honganji administration and was an important link between Kiyozawa and the Dobokai Movement. For information concerning his role in the Dobokai Movement, see the introduction to Chapter 3 and Text 18.

The Prajna-Paramita Sutra gives us the best explanation of what wisdom is. In this sutra, wisdom is explained in the words, 'All things are empty'. When we hear this, we might think that it means nothing exists, but the true meaning of emptiness, or nothingness, means no *kodawari* (attachment, rigidity, prejudice, preconception). In the state of nothingness, all problems are resolved: it is the state of flowing, as such. In Zen, we speak of nothingness, but this nothingness is not Void; it is the true reality. Therefore it is neither Being nor Void; it is the true state of being which transcends the dichotomy of Being and Void. It is that world of truth in which Being and Void are the same. This world is neither Being nor Void, yet it is both Being and Void. Being is Void and Void is Being. Yet there is no such Being to grasp nor Void to grasp. This world transcends both Being and Void.

In this world of nothingness, all the forms, all the concepts, all the opposites are unified when we see things as they are, which is the flowing of life itself. People think nothingness is Void, but as I say this is a wrong understanding. Nothingness, sunyata, is not void. Sunyata is sunyata. Void is void. They are different.

The so-called nothingness of nihilism or nihilistic is different from sunyata. Sunyata is not Void; sunyata is sunyata as reality. So if you ask me where sunyata is, I have to say, 'There is no such thing'. One cannot grasp it as such; that is the reality. When you grasp it as sunyata, then it is already Being, not sunyata. And sunyata as the state-of-not-being-grasped-as-it-is is wrong too. Because you have decided to describe sunyata as that which cannot be grasped, then, once again you have Being! Sunyata means that there is no such definite thing as Being and Void. There is no such fixed idea. The World, Life, Studies, the Law – there are no such things, as fixed entities. In the world of sunyata all things are living and moving, so we cannot grasp them as such. Once you grasp a thing, it is not sunyata. Truth changes continually; but after you decide that truth changes continually, it is already a concept, it is no longer the truth. So such a reality is not real. The world of sunyata is always moving, never fixed – a dynamic, living world.

Grasping at things is no good. Even with education – once you grasp it, then it is dead. So an educator should not teach too definitely that 'This is it'. Truth cannot be determined definitely. So do not give out with conclusions.

Very often we think that character or personality is definite – but there is no such definite character or personality in existence. Sometimes educators become stiffened up by thinking, 'I should embody virtue' but such people never give any real education. Their stiffness comes from being caught by concepts. Trying to be the body of virtue, their arms and legs get so stiff!

Trying to be the body of virtue, we kill ourselves. Because we are dead and unmoving, we can become a Model for others. A dead person does not move, a model does not move; no development, no change – he just stays still. This is why he has a fixed form. A living one will not have such a fixed form, for the very moment we decide 'This is it,' life changes. A living one hates to be tied to anything. A living one wants liberation. He hates to be caught by regulations and concepts. He wants to keep on changing forever. Sunyata means that all beings are living.

Even with truth, once we catch and grasp it, it is dead. Living things cannot be grasped. Whatever we catch is a dead body, a shell. Once we name truth, saying 'This is God,' or 'This is Buddha,' then it is no longer truth or God or Buddha.

In an aquarium, the goldfish swim as long as they are alive, but once we catch them, in order to explain, 'This is a goldfish,' then while we are talking the fish will die. A caught fish is a dead fish.

Once we open up to real wisdom, then we see the living truth as it is. There is infinite compassion. The real truth unfolds when we become one with ever-flowing reality itself. Real compassion means to see such a living, reverent being in all people, in all beings. When we awaken to this wisdom, we do not need God or Buddha. Those who are ignorant, their minds are in such darkness that wherever they go they are in the world of darkness. But in the world of wisdom all lives are leaping and dancing, and we live together with others, work together, enjoy together, worry together, yet all go on living our own lives. One who himself finds out such a life sees the whole world living such a life.

(*Shout of Buddha – Writings of Haya Akegarasu*, translated by Gyoko Saito & Joan Sweany (Orchid Press Publication, Chicago, Ill., 1977))
pp. 90-92

Text 10

Akegarasu Haya: *Mind of Embracing All Things*

Reading an early passage of the Kegon Sutra, I came across a poem by the Ho-E Bodhisattva which made me want to cry out, 'How Wonderful!' Here it is:

> Be free from subject and object,
> Get away from dirtiness and cleanness.
> Sometimes entangled and sometimes not,
> I forget all relative knowledge:
> My real wish is to enjoy all things with people.

This poem expresses so clearly what I am thinking about these days that I use it to explain my feelings to everyone I meet.

Subject or object, myself or someone else, individualism or socialism, egotism or altruism – forget about such relative knowledge, be freed from it! Right or wrong, good or bad, beauty or ugliness – don't cling to that either. Forget about ignorance or enlightenment! Simply enjoy your life with people – this is the spirit of Gautama Buddha, isn't it? I'm glad that Shinran Shonin said, 'When we enter into the inconceivable Other Power, we realize that the Reason without Reason does exist', and again, 'I cannot judge what right and wrong is, and I don't know at all what is good and bad.' I hate to hear about the fights of isms or clashes between two different faiths. I don't care about these things. Somehow I just long for people. I hate to be separated from people by the quarrels of ism or dogma or faith, and what is more, I hate to be separated from other people by profit and loss.

I don't care whether I win or lose, lose or win. I just long for the life burning inside me. I just adore people, in whom there is life. I don't care about isms, thoughts or faiths. I just long for people. I throw everything else away. I simply want people.

It makes me miserable when close brothers are separated by anything. Why can't they be their own naked selves? Why can't longing people embrace each other?

I love myself more than my isms, thoughts, or faiths. And because I love myself so, I long for people. I am not asserting that my way is Love-ism or Compassionate-Thinking-ism! Somehow I just can't keep myself in a little box of ism, thought or faith.

I must admit that I am timid. Because I am timid, I can't endure my loneliness. I want to enjoy everything with people.

> I go to the ocean of the great mind.
> I go to the mind of great power.

Once I hated people because they lived a lie; once I saw them as devils. Once I lamented because there was no one who cared about me. But now I long for them, even when they are devils and liars, even when they are evil. I don't care, I can't help it – I adore them! They breathe the same life that I do, even though they hate me, cheat me, make me suffer.

I am so filled with a thirst to adore people that there is no room in me for judging whether a person is good or bad, beautiful or ugly, right or wrong. This is not the result of something I reasoned out, such as that I live by being loved or by loving. Regardless of any ism, thought, or faith, I cannot be separated from people. Without reason or discussion, I just want to hug everyone! My missionary work is nothing but a confession of this mind.

(*Shout of Buddha – Writings of Haya Akegarasu*,
translated by Gyoko Saito & Joan Sweany,
(Orchid Press Publications,
Chicago, Ill. 1977)), pp. 167-68.

Text 11

Soga Ryojin: *Dharmakara Bodhisattva*

Soga Ryojin (1875-1971) was a colleague and friend of Kaneko Daiei and D.T. Suzuki at Otani University, and some of their talks have been written down and published in the Eastern Buddhist. *Like Kaneko, he was for a period excommunicated from the Shinshu denomination. Today his views are very much accepted, although some people consider him Zen-like in his outlook.*

Dharmakara is the bodhisattva name of Amida Buddha, see the General Introduction (part II).

It was in the sixth century that Buddhism came into Japan. Since then it has undergone gradual modifications, adapting itself to the particular historical and social situations in which it found itself. It went through a process of developing into many schools and sects, finally to become types of faith characteristically Japanese. Of all schools and sects, some are now to be counted among the past cultural assets of Japan, having discharged their respective missions as living religions. On the other hand, however, there are those schools that still now continue to be relevant to modern people as sources of religious inspiration. These schools include the Rinzai School of Zen Buddhism first introduced by Eisai (1141-1215), the Soto School of Zen Buddhism initiated by Dogen (1200-53), the Jodo School of Pure Land Buddhism started by Honen (1133-1212), the Jodo Shin School of Pure Land Buddhism started by Shinran (1173-1262), and the Nichiren School initiated by Nichiren (1222-82) together with its sub-schools which have now considerable influence over present-day society. The above-mentioned schools were all founded in the Kamakura Period (1192-1333). It may be said that, above all, Japanese Zen Buddhism is now well known all over the world, mainly due to the voluminous writings of Dr D.T. Suzuki. It is to be regretted, however, that the nature of Pure Land Buddhism as clarified by both Honen and Shinran is not yet known so widely or so rightly as Zen Buddhism.

Zen Buddhism teaches that we should develop our potential Buddha-nature to arrive at the realization in a flash of sudden Enlightenment that all sentient beings are by nature Buddhas. In Shingon Buddhism, it is taught that we can become Buddhas with our earthly bodies through the practice of the three-fold mystical union of body, speech and mind (*'sammitsu kaji'*). In Tendai Buddhism, the practices of concentration and contemplation are taught, and in Nichiren Buddhism the chanting of the formula of 'Namu Myō Hō Renge Kyō' is taught. Although the ways in which Enlightenment is sought are varied, they are all practices of self-effort aimed at attaining *prajñā* (Transcendental or undefiled Wisdom), the goal of Buddhism.

In contrast to the practices of the above-mentioned nature, Pure Land Buddhism teaches us to discard our dependence upon the practices of self-effort and instead to have faith solely in the Name-calling of 'Namu Amida Butsu' in order to be liberated by Amida or the Buddha of Infinite Light (Wisdom) and Eternal Life (Compassion). There are some people who criticize Pure Land Buddhism as being out of the mainstream of Buddhism. Exponents of Pure Land Buddhism such as Honen and Shinran, however, were deeply convinced that it was the way of Pure Land Buddhism which was truly conducive to the realization of the spirit of Mahayana Buddhism, which aims at enabling all sentient beings to become Buddhas. According to their conviction, it is impossible for all sentient beings to become Buddhas without realizing the depth of the Vow of Dharmākara Bodhisattva, the name of Amida in his disciplinary stage. All sentient beings are equally endowed with *prajñā* (Buddha-nature or faith) in a latent form as a cause for becoming Buddhas. It is the vow of Dharmākara Bodhisattva that wills to have all sentient beings awakened to this *prajñā* innate in them; and it is this *prajñā* which manifests itself as faith and in its working appears as the practice of the invocation of the Nembutsu as singled out by Dharmākara Bodhisattva in his Original Vow. This tenet was phrased by Shinran thus: 'The teaching of Jodo Shin Buddhism is that whosoever practices the Nembutsu believing in the Original Vow attains Buddhahood.'[1]

Therefore, to be saved by Amida means to be awakened to the depth of the Vow of Dharmākara Bodhisattva. Here I should like to point out that Dharmākara Bodhisattva appearing in the Pure Land teaching is by no means different from *ālayavijñāna* appearing in the traditional Mahayana doctrine, especially that of the Vijñānavādins. That is to say, the statement that Dharmākara Bodhisattva refers to *ālayavijñāna* should be a rejoinder by Pure Land Buddhism to its critics and this is meant for proving that Pure Land Buddhism is authentically Mahayana. In the statement that *ālayavijñāna* refers to Dharmākara Bodhisattva, it is implied that the fundamental principle of Mahayana Buddhism is actualized in this world as the realization of the Infinite in somebody 'personal'.

As mentioned above, there are some people who insist that Pure Land Buddhism is not in the authentic line of Buddhism, and that it is quite similar to Christianity, since it advocates salvation by Amida. As is apparent from the above, however, Amida is not a Transcendent Other standing over against sentient beings. Amida is not simply transcendent in the sense that he is externally transcendent to sentient beings. Amida is inherent in all sentient beings in His causal or Bodhisattva form called Dharmākara. Dharmākara Bodhisattva who is thus at once innate and transcendent to sentient beings becomes Amida, whereby their salvation is realized. Salvation by Amida is therefore not an heteronomous salvation by some Transcendent Other, but is a salvation attained the moment man is awakened to the depth of Dharmākara's Original Vow. To be awakened to the depth of the Original Vow means to acquire the enlightening Wisdom to know what one essentially is. The moment man is awakened to the depth of the Original Vow, the Enlightenment of Amida in the Pure Land (Transcendent Realm) is shared by him while remaining

---

1 The *Tannishō*, or *A Tract Deploring Heresies* by Yuien.

in this relative world – that is, his eventual attaining of Buddhahood is ensured.

□

The enlightened predecessors whom we look up to as ideal are all historical characters. They are all the projection of our respective ideals. They are our idealized teachers, but by no means our saviours. The real saviour for us is not our idealized historical characters but the universal self – the fundamental self upon which is based our actual self. The real saviour is Dharmākara Bodhisattva who does not exist apart from this physical body of mine as the fundamental subjectivity of myself. Manifesting himself in phenomenal bodies, Dharmākara Bodhisattva has become the living witness to his own actuality and thus deprives all futile arguments, illusions, dogmatisms, superstitions, doubts, procrastinations, controversies, and so forth of their foundations. Therefore he can be said to be a real saviour leading our life to truth.

Śākyamuni is our teacher, master, father, and ideal. Dharmākara Bodhisattva is the real person whom we can directly experience; he is our eternal actuality. It is no other than the preaching of our teacher, Śākyamuni, that urges us to hear the voice of Dharmākara Bodhisattva, that clarifies for us the Way through which we are to return to the undefiled, pure self.

Consequently, my way of understanding the teaching of the Jodo Shin School by Shinran is that it teaches us to realize the way of becoming a Buddha initially by pointing to the difference between 'teacher' and 'saviour'.

Eastern Buddhist, I/1 (1965), pp. 64-78
This article is reconstructed and adapted
by Emyo Ito and Shojun Bando from
Prof. Soga's writings in Japanese.

Text 12

Kaneko Daiei: *The Present Age and Our Present Situation*

*K*aneko Daiei (1881-1976), like Soga and Akegarasu the son of a
Shin priest, and like Soga and Suzuki teaching at Otani
University, was excommunicated in 1928 on grounds of heresy for his
strong criticism of the materialism he found in the Shinshu denomination,
but reinstated more that ten years later. Today, he is considered one of
the most important Shin thinkers.
This excerpt is from an article called 'Shin Religion as I Believe it'.

L astly, let me observe how the Shin followers take the present
age and men's present situation. Now, the Shin followers
claim their religion to be 'the only religion in conformity with the
times and men's capacities'. In these words is suggested their
awakened attitude towards the prevailing conditions of the times.
It may be said it is their sense of the times, which will constitute
the basis of their world view. We feel that we of the present age can
have no hope, neither within nor without. We have keenly felt this
these last ten years. We are living in an age when salvation is quite
impossible except by the Original Vow of Amida.

History moves beyond our will. As to the current of the times,
we cannot swim against it, nor can we remain its unconcerned
spectators. To swim against it is to lose one's life to no purpose,
while to remain its unconcerned spectators is to lose touch with
the times. And yet, the power of the times is actually controlling
us. We have no other way than follow it. We must say, therefore, if
the present situation does not permit us to live like human beings,
it is inevitable for us to live like an animal. We have no choice.
Argumentations are all idle talk.

However, we Nembutsu followers cannot but feel that we are
sinful, for it is indeed due to our karma that we are destined to live
in an age such as this. And our view of sin consists in proving
ourselves blameable. We ourselves are blameable, because we
ourselves are through our own karma the makers of all the evils of
the times. Here we are convinced that we ought not to take
advantage of the times. Those who do so seize every opportunity
afforded by the times and busy themselves in making money and

54

in gaining honours. The so-called ideologies are advocated from the same motive. But these are doings of men who do not believe in the Eternally True World. We who are awakened to its presence will do nothing but obey the dictate of the times and do what we think the best in the circumstances under which we are placed. And this 'best' does exist even in the animal-like existence. The practice of the Nembutsu will open the way for us to go serenely. In this sense, it may be said that the Nembutsu followers are given the freedom that knows no obstacle in any age whatever.

But it is due to the fact that they always concentrate their minds on the serenity of cessation (Nirvana) even while they are obedient to the dictate of the times, that the Nembutsu followers are thus blessed with the way of freedom. Sakyamuni, who had his mind set upon Nirvana, said: 'I do not contend with the world, neither do I become defiled by the world.' All the systems of thoughts hinge on the attachment of life. But the Buddhist doctrine rests on the serenity of cessation of life. The doctrine of this kind may not directly lay down how society should be; but, if society disregards this kind of doctrine, it will not be able to stand strong and firm. For this reason, I should like to say, with Shinran the founder of Shin Buddhism, 'Peace be reigned in the world, and Dharma be diffused.'

From *The Eastern Buddhist*, vol. VIII, no. 2 (May 1951), pp. 40-42.

Daisetz T. Suzuki

Text 13

D.T. Suzuki: *The Shin Teaching of Buddhism*

*D*aisetz T. Suzuki (1870-1966) is the best known conveyor of *Japanese Buddhism to the West. His lifelong efforts have been mentioned in the 'Preface' and the introduction to chapter 2 – on 'Shin Buddhism in the Modern Age'. His collected works in Japanese number 32 volumes and in English about 30.*

He was born in Kanazawa and studied at Tokyo University at the same time as he undertook Zen training at Engakuji, Kamakura, under Shaku Soen (1859-1919). Due to Soen's participation in the World's Parliament of Religions in 1893 and his meeting there with Dr Paul Carus, D.T. Suzuki was sent to America in 1897 to assist in the planned translations of Oriental philosophical and religious works. He returned to Japan in 1909, was a lecturer and later professor at Gakushuin University until he in 1921 became professor of Buddhist philosophy at Otani University, Kyoto. In 1911 he married Beatrice Lane who became his close collaborator until her death in 1939.

Suzuki's most influential work was 'Zen Buddhism and Its Influence on Japanese Culture' (1938) which made many Westerners think of him as exclusively Zen. But all his life he stressed the essential oneness of Mahayana Buddhism. For instance, when asked by the well-known English potter, Bernard Leach, to explain his interest in Shin Buddhism as opposed to his concentration on Zen, he answered: 'If you think there is a division, you have not begun to understand – there is no dualism in Buddhism.'

The essential oneness must be understood, also when Suzuki in the following text and in text 15 draws attention to some differences.

---

*B*oth Jōdo and Shin belong to the Pure Land School. Jōdo means the 'Pure Land' and the official title of the Shin is Jōdo Shin and not just Shin. *Shin* means 'true' and its devotees claim that their teaching is truly *tariki* whereas the Jōdo is not quite so, being mixed with the *jiriki* idea: hence *Shin* 'true' added to Jōdo.

The main points of difference between the Jōdo and the Shin teaching are essentially two: 1. Jōdo fully believes with Shin in the efficacy of Amida's Vow but thinks that Amida's Name is to be repeatedly recited; whereas Shin places its emphasis upon faith and not necessarily upon the nembutsu,[1] which is the repeated recitation of the Name. 2. Jōdo encourages good works as helpful for the devotee being born in the Pure Land; whereas Shin finds here a residue of the jiriki ('self-power') and insists that as long as the devotee awakens his wholehearted faith in Amida, Amida will take care of him unconditionally, absolutely assuring his entrance into the Pure Land. Whatever nembutsu he may offer to Amida it is no more than the grateful appreciation of the favour of the Buddha.

The fundamental idea underlying the Shin faith is that we as individual existences are karma-bound and therefore sinful, for karma is inevitably connected with sin; that as no karma-bound beings are capable of effecting their own emancipation, they have to take refuge in Amida who out of his infinite love for all beings is ever extending his helping arms; and that all that is needed of us is to remain altogether passive towards Amida, for he awakens in our hearts, when they are thoroughly purged of all the ideas of self and self-reliance, a faith which at once joins us to Amida and makes us entirely his. This being so, we as creatures subject to the law of moral causation can accomplish nothing worthy of the Pure Land; all good works so called are not all good from the viewpoint of absolute value, for they are always found deeply tinged with the idea of selfhood which no relatively-conditioned beings are able to shake off. Amida, in his capacity of Infinite Light and Eternal Life, stands against us, ever beckoning us to cross the stream of birth-and-death. Faith is the act of response on our part, and its practical result is our crossing the stream.

(*Collected Writings on Shin Buddhism*,
(Shinshu Otaniha, Kyoto, 1973), p. 51)

---

1 In Sanskrit, *buddhasmṛti*, literally, 'thinking of the Buddha'. But it has come to be synonymous with *shōmyō*, 'reciting or pronouncing the Name'. For the Jōdo followers *nembutsu* means *shōmyō*, to think of the Buddha is to pronounce his Name, Amida. For further remarks see below and also my *Essays in Zen Buddhism*, Series II (London: Luzac and Company, 1933), pp. 129 et seq.

Text 14

D.T. Suzuki: *Shin Buddhism and Christianity Compared*

*F*or an introduction to D.T. Suzuki, see the preceding text.

With regard to Christianity, Suzuki was especially interested in Christian mysticism. In Mysticism: Christian and Buddhist *(1957) he focuses on Meister Eckhart and the Buddhist myokonin. [See Text 25 in this book.]*

A comparison with Christianity may help us to understand the characteristic teaching of Shin as a development of the Pure Land doctrine and also as a school of Mahāyāna Buddhism, however strangely formed at first sight it may appear. The following points of difference may be observed as existing between Buddhism and Christianity.

1. Amida to all appearances may be regarded as corresponding to the Christian notion of God. Amida however is not the creator, nor is he to be considered the author of evil in this world, which inevitably follows from the notion of creatorship.

Whatever evils there are in this world, they are all our own doings, for everything karma-conditioned individuals can do is necessarily evil and has no merit entitling them to appear before Amida. This polarization of Amida and individual beings (*sarvasattva*) is one of the specific features of Shin thought. In this respect its followers may be said to be transcendentalists or dualists.

Amida is the pure embodiment of love. Whoever believes in him as saviour is sure of being taken up by Amida and sent to his Pure Land. Amida's love makes no distinction between evil-doers and good men, because as Shinran says there is no evil strong enough to prevent one's being embraced in Amida's infinite love, nor is there any good in this world which is so perfect and pure as to permit its agent into the Land of Purity without resorting to the Original Vow. We who belong to this world of relativity are always conscious of what we are doing, for we are so constituted and cannot be otherwise. When we do something good, we become conscious of it, and it is this very consciousness that destroys the merit of goodness. The being conscious of something comes out of the idea of selfhood, and there is nothing more effective than the idea of selfhood which will disqualify one as candidate for the Pure Land of Amida. The unqualified acceptance of the *tariki* is what leads to the presence of the infinitely loving one. For this reason, as long as we are creatures of the world conscious of its relative values, we lose the right to be with Amida and his hosts. Good men cease to be good as soon as they become conscious of their goodness and attempt to make something out of it; evil-doers have their sins eradicated and become worthy of the Pure Land at the very moment they are illumined by Amida's light: for Amida is a kind of melting-pot of good and evil, in which faith alone retains its absolute value. Not being the creator, Amida has no idea to discipline beings. He is the Light of Love shared universally by all beings. However bad they are, Amida knows that it is due to their karma and that this never proves to be a hindrance to their entering the Pure Land. What he demands of them is faith. This keeping Amida away from responsibilities of this dualistic world marks out Shin as a unique religious teaching.

2. In Christianity, God requires a mediator to communicate with his creatures and this mediator is sacrificed for the sake of the latter whose sins are too dark to be wiped of by their own efforts. God demands an innocent victim in order to save souls who are not necessarily responsible for their unrighteousness because they are born so. This proceeding does not seem to be quite fair on the part of God, but the Christian experience has demonstrated at least its pragmatic value. In Shin, Amida performs in a sense the office of God and also that of Christ. Amida with Amidists is Light (*ābha*) and Life (*āyus*) and Love (*karuṇā*), and from his Love and Life issue his vows, and it is through these vows that Amida is connected with us. The Vow is mediator, and as it emanates from Amida's Love, it is just as efficient as Christ in its office of mediatorship. One thing we must observe here is that in Christianity concrete images are made use of while in Shin words and phrases, more or less abstract in a sense, are given out to do the work of a mediating agent, as is exemplified in *Namu-amida-butsu*.

3. The Christians like to think that their religion is based on historical facts while Buddhism, especially Shin, is a metaphysical reconstruction, so to speak, of the ideas and aspirations which generally make up a religion. For this reason, Christianity to its

followers is more solidly and objectively constituted. Here is one of the fundamental differences – indeed the fundamental difference – between Christianity and Shin. Shin in accordance with the general make-up of Buddhism is not dualistically minded, however much it may appear so superficially; moreover it does not take very kindly to the idea that objectivity is more real than subjectivity. Truth is neither subjective nor objective, there is no more reality in what is known as historical fact than in what is considered psychological or metaphysical. In some cases historicity is mere fiction. History takes place in time, and time as much as space depends upon our intellectual reconstruction. Religious faith, however, wants to grasp what is not conditioned by time and space, it wishes to take hold of what is behind historical facts. And this must be Reality transcending the polarization of subject and object. History is karmic, and Shin aspires after the akarmic or that which is not historical.

Amida is above karma, he is not of history, he is akarmic; that is to say, all historical facts, all karmic events have their origin in Amida and return to him, he is the alpha and omega of all things. From him, therefore, are all his vows taking effect in the world of karma where we sentient beings have our temporal and spatial abode. Some may say that Amida is too metaphysical to be an object of religious consciousness which requires a concrete and tangible historical person. To this Shin would answer: As long as we are on the time-plane of relativity, we may distinguish between metaphysical and historical, between abstract ideas and concrete events; but in genuine religious faith once realized, there are no such discriminations to be made, for faith is attained only when there is the going-beyond of a world of contrasts, which is the leaping over the gap of dualism.

4. There is no crucifixion in Shin, which is significant in more ways than one. I presume that the crucified Christ is the symbol of self-sacrifice for the Christians, but at the same time to see the figure of crucifixion on the altar or by the country roadside is not a very pleasant sight, at least to the Buddhist. The sight, to tell the truth, is almost the symbol of cruelty or of inhumanity. The idea of washing sin with the blood of Christ crucified reminds us of the primitive barbarism of victim-offering to the gods. The association of sin and blood is not at all Buddhistic.

> 'I am saved by the blood
> Of the Crucified One.'

This will never awaken in the Buddhist heart a sacred exalted feeling as in the Christian. The agony of crucifixion, death, and resurrection making up the contents of Christian faith, have significance only when the background impregnating old tradition is taken into consideration, and this background is wholly wanting in Buddhists who have been reared in an atmosphere different not only historically but intellectually and emotionally. Buddhists do not wish to have the idea of self-sacrifice brought before their eyes in such bloody imagery.

The Buddhist idea of death is rest and peace, and not agony. The Buddha at his Nirvāṇa lies quietly on his bed surrounded by all beings including the birds of the air and the beasts of the field. His horizontal posture is a great contrast to Christ on the cross. The Buddha is again represented as sitting in meditation, symbol of eternal tranquillity.

5. The Christian notion of vicarious atonement may be considered corresponding to the Buddhist notion of merit-transference (*pariṇāmana*), but the difference is that somebody in one case is to be sacrificed for the fault of others, while in the other case it is merit accumulated by the Bodhisattva that is desired to be transferred to other beings. As far as the fact of transference is concerned, there is an analogy between the Christian and the Buddhist, but the analogy stops here. In Buddhism, naturally including Shin, the idea is positive and creative in the sense that value produced in one quarter of the universe is made to spread all over it so that the whole creation may advance towards Enlightenment. Strictly speaking, there is no idea of atonement in Buddhism, especially in Shin – which makes indeed the position of Shin unique in the various systems of Mahāyāna Buddhist philosophy.

Amida, according to the teaching of Shin, has no intention to interfere with the working of karma, for it has to run its course in this world, the debt incurred by one person is to be paid by him and not by another. But the mysterious power of Amida's Name and Vow – which is the mystery of life to be simply accepted as such, all the logical contradictions notwithstanding – lifts the offender from the curse of karma and carries him to the Land of Purity and Happiness, where he attains his supreme enlightenment. While karma is left to itself, what is beyond the reach of karma which may be termed the akarmic power of Buddha, is working quite unknowingly to the karma-bearer himself. But he begins to realize this fact as soon as faith in Amida is awakened in him. Faith works this miracle in his consciousness. Although he knows that he is subject to the law of karma and may have to go on in spite of himself, committing deeds of karma, his inmost consciousness, once his faith is established, tells him he is bound for Amida's Land at the end of his karmic life on this earth. It is by this inmost consciousness in the Shin devotee that the truth of merit-transference (*pariṇāmana*) is demonstrated. In a similar way Christians feel assured of vicarious atonement when their faith is confirmed in Christ. Whatever theological and ethical interpretation may be given to this, the truth or fact, psychologically speaking, remains the same with Christians and Buddhists: it is the experience of a leap from the relative plane of consciousness to the Unconscious.

Crucifixion, death, resurrection, and ascension – these are all really the contents of individual religious experience regardless of difference in philosophical reconstruction. Different religions may use different terminology which is the product mainly of intellectual antecedents. To the Shin Buddhists, resurrection and ascension will mean rebirth in the Pure Land and Enlightenment while crucifixion and death will correspond to the death, that is, abandoning of 'self-power' (*jiriki*). That the abandoning of self-power is death is a well-known experience with Shin followers, and it is at this moment that they utter from the depths of their being the '*Namu-amida-butsu*'. This utterance, given just once, of Amida's Name puts an end to all their sufferings and agonies of the beginningless past and they are born in Amida's Pure Land. Their bodily existence as far as they are conscious of it will continue in the world of karma, but as their faith tells them, they already belong to another world. The Christians may not agree with this form of interpretation, they may like to ascribe all such experiences to Christ himself while their individual human salvation is regarded to come from believing in supernatural events. This is quite natural with the genius of the Jewish tradition. Even when they say 'to die in Adam and to live in Christ', I wonder if by this they mean our going through all the spiritual experiences individually and personally of Christ himself, instead of our merely believing in Christ as divine mediator.

(*Collected Writings on Shin Buddhism*,
(Shinshu Otaniha, Kyoto, 1973), p. 57-61)

Text 15

D.T. Suzuki: *Shinran and Søren Kierkegaard*

*F*or an introduction to D.T. Suzuki, see Text 13.

Søren Kierkegaard (1813-55) is the great Danish philosopher, who as a religious thinker maintained that there is no way of reaching faith through reason and that faith is always a jump into what you cannot be sure of. As a philosopher Kierkegaard was one of the main sources of inspiration of modern existentialism.

An important point not only in Shin but in all Mahāyāna Buddhism is that salvation is universal; there are no beings on whom the light does not shine; all may awake to enlightenment. This being the fact, Shinran appeals to us to take refuge in the True Light which is Amitābha.

But how are we to take refuge through faith in Amida's power to save? To get this faith is not so easy as one might think and as is claimed by teachers of Shin. There has to be a strong effort to obtain it. So in the end it may be as difficult as the efforts of Self-power sect believers.

To obtain this faith corresponds to conversion among the Christians. According to Shinran's own explanation, the experience should be sudden, *ōchō* as he called it. *Ōchō* means 'to leap crosswise' and may be contrasted to Zen's 'straightforward leap'. Both Zen and Shin belong to what is known as the 'abrupt school'. The progress made in the understanding of the truth is not gradual, not going from step to step as is done in logic but it is a leap over the gap. You come to the end of your journey, you halt and are at a loss how to make further advance as there is before you a gaping abyss. Zen jumps straight forward while Shin jumps crosswise. The line of Zen suggests continuous extension and according to Shin is not quite a leap in its proper sense. What Shin accomplishes is really discontinuous, proving that the deed springs from the 'other power'[1] which is Amida.

This is similar to what the Christian philosopher Søren Kierkegaard[2] calls the Leap and the Instant. In his *Philosophical Fragments* he says: 'And now the Instant! Such an instant has a peculiar character. It is short indeed and temporal, as every instant is fleeting, as every instant is, gone like all instants, the following instant, and yet it is decisive, and yet it is full of eternity. Such an instant must have a special name, let us call it *the fullness of time.*' (Walter Lowrie – *Kierkegaard*, p. 312.) Shin would call it the fullness of faith.

And again Kierkegaard says: 'Religious faith is not to be reached by any approximations of proof and probability but only by a leap.'

(*Collected Writings on Shin Buddhism*,
(Shinshu Otaniha, Kyoto, 1973), p. 117)

Text 16

Hirose Takashi:
Shinran's Ideas of Equality

Former president of Otani University, Hirose Takashi (b. 1924) in this text argues for the social dimension in Shinran's thoughts.

People always talk about equality, dealing with the subject in various ways. What is most important, however, is where one places oneself when addressing this problem – for equality to mean anything, it must be examined from a clearly defined position. Shinran does not merely say that all men are equal, an abstraction so vague as to be meaningless. The equality that Shinran spoke of was the tangible, down-to-earth equality he discovered in the life he led among fishermen, hunters, merchants, and farmers. This, I feel, is an important point to bear in mind.

---

1 'Other power': Shin makes the distinction between *tariki* and *jiriki*. *Jiriki* means 'self-power' or depending on one's own virtues for rebirth in the Pure Land while *tariki*, literally 'other-power', is to put oneself in a state of complete passivity and losing self altogether in the other, i.e., Amida. Zen according to Shin is *jiriki* and Shin is pure *tariki*.

2 Søren Kierkegaard, religious philosopher of Denmark, born 1813, died 1855. He had through his writings a great influence on many modern philosophers and religionists.

Moreover, something far stronger and more affirmative than mere sympathy for these down-trodden people lies behind Shinran's assessment. Living in the midst of people from the lowest ranks of society prompted Shinran to critically re-evaluate the values of traditional Buddhism, that is, Buddhism before Hōnen.

Traditional Buddhism tells us that we are born as human beings by virtue of our having obeyed the Buddhist precepts in our previous lives, and thus we should continue maintaining these precepts throughout this life as well. The Buddhist precepts (against killing, stealing, adultery, lying, and taking intoxicants) are of course extremely important. What Shinran realized in his life among the common people of Echigo, though, was that if the maintenance of these precepts was prerequisite to the Buddhist life, then Buddhism could play no meaningful part in the lives of ordinary men and women. Fishermen and hunters made their livelihood through the taking of life; the role of the merchant almost inevitably involved a certain amount of duplicity, even theft of a kind. The lot of the farmers was little better. In the feudalistic system of Shinran's time, farmers were just manpower for working the landlord's fields. It was considered theft if they set aside any of the crop for their own use. The situation was made even worse by the fact that the landowner was often a powerful Buddhist temple or Shinto shrine: to withhold from them was the equivalent of stealing from the coffers of a church.

Thus the common people of Shinran's time were virtually forced to break the precepts in order to survive. This must have caused Shinran to re-examine the validity and meaning of traditional Buddhist values. Were these people any less human for breaking the precepts? Shinran's soul-searching examination forced him to the conclusion that far from being less human, it was actually they who were living life as it had to be lived in the real world. The upper classes, the patrons and followers of traditional Buddhism who held the common people in contempt, were the ones who were separated from reality, living of the backbreaking labour of the poor. If the common people were to be excluded from salvation, then perhaps it would be best to abandon Buddhism.

Shinran realized, however, that this view of Buddhism was flawed. True Buddhism teaches that all living beings are possessed of Buddha-nature and promises the awakening of all mankind.

Among the writings of Shinran is the following verse:

The plea of the rich
　is like a stone going into water:
The plea of the poor
　is like water going into stone.

When the rich make a plea in court, the matter quickly reaches a favourable conclusion, just like a stone entering the water. When the poor make a plea, though, the court is reluctant to take up the case, and, even if it does, a favourable outcome is rarely forthcoming. For the poor, it is like trying to put water into a stone.

This verse indicates Shinran's recognition of the fact that the desperate plight of the common people was caused by the very structure of feudal society, including the traditional Buddhism which was such an important part of that structure. With this recognition Shinran ascertained the absolute equality of all humanity within the law of karmic conditioning, expressing this insight in the previously quoted phrase: 'If our karmic conditions were such, there is nothing we wouldn't do.'

This truth, profound beyond human comprehension, is at the source of man's basic equality. When we awaken to this equality, when we awaken to our true nature as human beings, then the bonds of social systems and structures are transcended and we are born to the life in which all men, all living beings, exist in mutually sustaining harmony. Any teaching which is unable to lead men to this living reality cannot be called Buddhism.

(*Lectures on Shin Buddhism*, (Higashi Honganji,
Kyoto, 1980), p. 47-51

3 The Dobokai Movement

In Japan, all the established religions were weakened after the Pacific War (1941-45). Not only State Shinto but also Buddhist denominations, Christianity and some new religions had supported the nationalist governments. After the defeat many people in Japan turned away from religions or turned to those new religions which did not have such a past or who had been persecuted by the state. In the fifties and sixties it was especially Soka Gakkai, the lay movement of Nichiren Shoshu, which made great strides. It is characteristic that the established Buddhist sects were treated with strong criticism in journals of religion and books in the sixties, which prophesied their rapidly declining influence.

The decline has not taken place, however. Some of the religions, including Shinshu Otaniha, have set up reform movements to meet the threat. In Otaniha the reform movement found inspiration in the Meiji reformer, Kiyozawa Manshi (1863-1903), who in his time also fought against a conservative clergy and a feudal abbot. Akegarasu Haya was a Kiyozawa disciple and the direct inspirer of the Dobokai movement.

Dobo means 'brother (in faith)' and *kai* 'assembly', and the movement is an attempt to educate the laity and bridge the gap between popular beliefs and the new thinkers in Shin Buddhism. According to further information from the Dobokaikan, the centre at Higashi Honganji (Otaniha), the movement climaxed around 1968 when 30,000 followers annually received training. The figure decreased gradually until 1986 when the movement was given a new impetus, especially by educating instructors or propagators. In 1993 the number of people who undergo training at the Dobokaikan is 10,000 annually and 14,000 when followers attending local centres are included. The number is rising again.

To describe Shinshu Otaniha today it must be added that the power of the former head of the sect, Otani Kocho (1903-93), who was the 24th hereditary successor of Shinran, was severely reduced. He was in conflict with the democratically elected administration dominated by a reform movement. This was due to financial scandals, especially, for which the Otani family have been held responsible. It led to lawsuits and a new constitution which makes the power of the head of the Otani family purely symbolic. Otani Kocho died in 1993. After an interlude in which the grandson, Otani Narishige (b.1973), was meant to be the new successor, the Otani denomination installed Otani Choken (b. 1930), third son of Otani Kocho, as the 25th successor of Shinran in November 1996. The 67-year-old Otani Choken has an auditory handicap which, according to Shin Buddhists, promotes his understanding and sympathy for the weak.

It is natural to compare the role of the hereditary monarchical abbacy with that of the Japanese Emperor in present-day Japan, as a symbol of the unity of the country or, in this case, the denomination. Incidentally, the Otani family is closely related to the Imperial family, but historically the feudal power of the Otani family is a fairly modern invention stemming from a centralization of power in the Meiji era. The same is true of the Nishi Honganji denomination as well.

Opponents of the family like to quote Shinran himself for not wanting any personal heir: 'I have not a single disciple'. But the hereditary priesthood, which the conflict rests on, is not to be changed, not even by the reform movement.

Text 17

The Goal of the Shinshu Dobo-Kai Movement

The Dobo-kai movement was begun on the occasion of the 700th memorial of Shinran Shonin on 1962 to bring together each and every member of the Higashi Honganji in the spirit of the teaching of Shinran Shonin. This movement for religious awakening was installed to restore the spirit of Mahayana Buddhism through the fundamental teaching of Shinran Shonin based on the Primal Vow of Amida Buddha. Since then, for the past thirty years, the movement has continued to be shared by many members of the Higashi Honganji Sangha.

In the conclusion of Shinran's major work, *The Kyogyoshinsho,* he states:

Dobo kaikan, at Higashi Honganji

My wish is that those who have attained Birth may lead those who come after them, and those who aspire for Birth may follow their predecessors, thus following one after another endlessly and uninterruptedly until the boundless sea of birth and death is exhausted.

This 'endless and uninterrupted' wish is the foundation of the Shinshu Dobo-kai Movement, and is the power behind our efforts to move forward. We who have had the good fortune of encountering the Shinshu teaching have been entrusted with the responsibility to transmit that teaching to the next generations.

We live in societies that have become more and more complex and diversified. On the one hand, life-styles have become more comfortable and convenient. But such 'progress' has replaced cultures of spiritualism with materialism, and has resulted in wholesale changes in the family structure. We enjoy materialistic abundance on the one hand, but greater numbers suffer from a general feeling of anxiety about life and a sense of isolation.

We see today the increase in secularized religions that cater to such anxieties with prayer or with quick solutions to the sufferings of the people.

It is in this time-frame that our Shinshu Otani-ha denomination took the initiative to reevaluate the Shinshu Dobo-kai Movement in 1988 by returning to the original motivation of its beginning. New educational programmes, one called '*Suishin-in Yosei Koza*', an intensive study programme on the local district level, and another called '*Gomeinichi no Tsudoi*', a more informal meeting once a month on the memorial date of Shinran Shonin on the local temple level, were begun to the wide acceptance and participation of many Sangha members. The objective of the Shinshu Dobo-kai is to create a true Sangha of people living together in harmony based on the one path of Nembutsu. It is the creation of a place where people can lay bare their anxieties, where people can listen together to the Dharma to discover the true meaning of living as human beings.

The monthly gatherings on Shinran Shonin's memorial on the 28th day can give us the opportunity to gather together at our temples to listen to teachings to overcome the uneasiness we have about life. At the same time, it is to encounter the long tradition that was created over hundreds of years by countless numbers of members of our Sangha. May we continue this tradition 'endlessly and uninterruptedly' to promote the ideals of the Shinshu Dobokai Movement as we prepare for the 500th-year Memorial of Rennyo Shonin.

It is very appropriate and meaningful that we hold this 6th World Dobo Convention at the site where Rennyo lived and endeavoured. That era saw a Japan that was severely divided, but through his efforts, people from everywhere transcended those boundaries to create a single Sangha based on a 'Nembutsu that brought people together'. The progress that was made 500 years ago in Japan is now in the process of occurring on a global scale.

Let us carry on the wishes of the previous convention in Hawai'i three years ago that began with the words: 'We open this convention with the wish that the Nembutsu can become a teaching for people everywhere, transcending differences in national boundaries, languages, cultures and beliefs.' May this convention be a first step in reconfirming our conviction to work towards this goal as we head toward the 21st Century.

(The 6th World Dobo Convention, Higashi
Honganji, 1992)

Text 18

The Dobokai Movement – an Interview

Interview with Mr Fujinaga Shunko of the training section of the Dobokai on 13 October 1992, at the Dobokaikan.

Tapescript of questions and answers translated by Prof. Yasutomi Shinya, Otani University.

Q: First let us talk about the background of the *dobokai*-movement and the reasons for setting up the movement in 1962.
A: As an administrative thing it started in 1962 but it is traceable to 1947 when the faith-movement started in the name of *shinjinsha*, a 'true person community'. At that time the Pacific War was finally over and it was a period of great devastation in economic and spiritual matters. At that time the religious community itself was confronted with the crisis of how to continue. It was then that the shinjinsha started, when *dobo* (brethren) was a kind of slogan. If the Higashi Honganji had not taken up the challenge, it would have meant the end of the

religious community. So the faith-movement began with about 290 priests who came together to mark the start of the *shinjinsha*. While searching for the direction the new movement should go, at the anniversary in 1949, Haya Akegarasu, when he was head of the administration of the Higashi Honganji, started the '*dobo* living movement', the *dobo seikatsu*. At that time Akegarasu said in his famous announcement to the members of Jodoshinshu: 'First *shinjin*, second *shinjin* and third *shinjin*.' Faith created the direction. Concretely, this was the real start of the *dobokai* movement. Not 1962.

Q: How was the decision received by the established religious community, at the head temple and the district temples within the Higashi Honganji?
A: Whether or not it was accepted, Akegarasu himself went out to the temples to fulfil his wish for the movement. He did not stay in his chair. But there was a conflict with the old ideas of Jodoshinshu and the new ideas of Jodoshinshu. The old ideas are the feudalistic ideas, the conservative ideas that the 'pure land' is only after death. But Kiyozawa Manshi's ideas were that the pure land is not after death, but in the present life. The pure land exists in our minds. We are assured of faith in this life. So there was a difference regarding the understanding of *shinshu* at that time.

Q: Was the new movement a grassroots movement?
A: (laughter) Yes, you can say that, but it changed from being a family religion to a religion for the awakening of the individual.

Q: You mentioned Kiyosawa Manshi before. And I realize that the *Tannisho* is the important background of the *dobokai* movement. Isn't that true?
A: It played a very big role, it was the basis of the movement. The *Tannisho* means the 'deploring of differences', a deploring of the spiritual differences.

Q: If we move on to the movement today, I have first some practical questions. Who organizes the *dobo* training? Head temple? Betsuin (district temples)? Or both?
A: The central body of the dobokai movement is at the head temple, but the movement is realized at each individual temple. The aim of the *dobokai* movement is to have *dobokai* in each temple.

Q: Also village temples?
A: Yes. But in the individual temples there are a lot of limitations of how to 'produce' nembutsu people.

Q: And there are difficulties in the small temples?
A: Yes, but the movement means to create nembutsu people also in small village temples.

Q: I understand that the movement is a lay movement, but how do you organize their stays at the *dobokaikan* here, for instance.
A: Each temple has its own assembly with meetings, dharma meetings. The participants of these meetings consult the priest if they want to have some training. That is, they apply for a training period.

Q: Is there any selection procedure?
A: There is a council of three members chosen among introducers, teachers and lecturers. The stays are two nights and three days where they are given some orientation and they have some questions. According to the questions they ask to share this teaching of the scriptures.

Q: Are there longer sessions than 2-3 days?
A: Almost all are only here for 2-3 days as the next group is waiting to start.

Q: Do you have any statistics of how many people receive this training?
A: Per year the number is about 14,000 and from 200 to 800 groups come.

Q: Is the number growing or is it decreasing?
A: It is increasing.

Q: To what extent are temple priests involved?
A: Here priests are working as *mompo-sha* (truth seekers), about 150 priests and 180 young instructors and assistants who have not yet finished their education.

Q: What is the women's role in the movement?
A: There is no discrimination or selection according to whether they are female or male. But if they have a certificate as teachers

and priests, that is the basis of the selection.

Q: And what about the lay people who come. Are they mostly men or mostly women?
A: About 60 per cent are male and 40 per cent are female.

Q: What are the age groups of people coming?
A: The average age is 55-57.

Q: Now some questions about the relationship with the head temple. What is the place of the movement in the constitution? Where does it fit in with the lay council and the priests' council?
A: There is only one faith movement in the Higashi Honganji and it is the *dobokai* movement. How the movement works is discussed in the 'parliament' set up by the constitution.

Q: The parliament has two chambers. One for lay people and one for priests.
A: Both discuss the politics of the movement and the outcome of the discussions is reflected in the movement.

Q: What is the influence of the movement on these two councils?
A: The dobokai movement has two sides. One is education, the other is philosophy. Or theological and educational aspects. The movement very much influences the theology of Jodoshinshu. And the *dobokai* movement especially reflects the lay council.

Q: What is the relationship between the *dobo* society and the present *kancho* (Otani Kocho, 1903-93)?
A: The *kancho* is a symbol of the religious community. Because he is a symbol he is not responsible for the policies of Jodoshinshu. We want the *kancho* to be the first propagator of the dobokai movement, that is the wish of our community. He is not the teacher of the faith but the first hearer of the faith. He is the person who sits in the front seat.

Q: What is your evaluation of the success of the movement. Have you reached your goals?
A: There are no specific goals – as long as people come here. It is 30 years since the movement had its official start. At that time the subject of discussion was the economic growth of the country and the new religions. After 30 years the family patterns in Japan have

greatly changed. The families then had a fixed pattern but today it has become the nuclear family. And even the nuclear family is at the point of collapse. In this situation the question of individuality becomes more important. The movement in the future should focus on the individual person. So we have started a series of lectures about the progress of the dobokai movement.

Q: And this is the new trend in the movement?
A: Yes. And the selection of instructors and propagators. How to create new progress.

Q: Do you see the new religions as growing or decreasing?
A: The rise of the new religions is typical for the Japanese social climate and is an expression of the belief in spirits. Jodoshinshu denies such belief in spirits. Japanese Buddhism has its own doctrines, how to deal with the belief in spirits, which forms the primitive religious soil of Japan.

Q: My last question: Is it possible to see the dobokai movement as an expression of Self Power and not Other Power (*tariki*)? Is there a theological problem here? A problem that people help themselves by being dobokai members?
A: We cannot produce anything by our own effort. By transmitting the dharma to people, we can awaken the Other Power. That is to say that every human being exists in dependent origination. When people encounter the teaching, we may awaken the Other Power.

Q: So it is to clear the ground for the Other Power to come?
A: We can only offer the grounds, we can only create the possibilities.

Q: And the rest is up to the Other Power?
A: Yes.

Text 19

Manual for Propagators of the Dobokai Movement

INTRODUCTION

As agreed upon in the present religious constitution from Showa 56 (1981) and carried out when Shinshu Otani-ha merged organizationally with (Higashi) Honganji in December Showa 62 (1987):

> Give expression to the faith you represent confidently and continually – be a witness of *doboshakai*.

In this way our religious organization shall always endeavour to realize the true spirit of the *dobokai* movement. At the organizational level our religious community has in reality made good the unrest which ruled persistently since April Showa 44 (1969).

Now the time has come for our religious organization to take a new step in the encounter with the 21st century, as it strongly supports the *dobokai* movement, which is the real centre of our organization.

The following quotation from Shinran Shonin's *Kyogyoshinsho* underlines this:

> The first-born shall show the way to those born later, and the latest born shall seek advice from those born earlier. In this way I want it to continue without interruption. It follows from the law of giving oneself over to the limitless ocean of birth and death.

This mentality has been the basis of the Shinshu organization and has been passed on for more than 700 years. On the historical background of today's Jodoshinshu we have come to know this wonderfully deep and wide wish, and are embraced by a glorious providence. This treasure we must hand over to the next generation.

But because modern man only trusts himself and seeks progress and prosperity, he loses his innermost being, lives a 'life without death' and staggers along with unspeakable inner unrest and anxiety. The unrest and pain of modern man once more makes topical the *dobokai* theme: 'From a family religion to an individual religion of awakening.' In other words, individual enlightenment. But 'individual' in the phrase 'individual awakening' often ends in modern egotism and is difficult to develop into true 'individual awakening' (*ko no jikaku*) the way Shin Buddhism wants it. What is gaining ground today is the attitude that uses religion to fulfil needs and gain happiness; a sort of worldly religiosity that uses religion to flee from what is unpleasant. In this religious trend the will to peace of mind is blurred and the meaning of true religion is lost.

In this serious situation in our time the opposite teachings are of course of enormous importance, that is to listen, to acquire and to receive the true teachings on the meaning of life. Concerning this the phrase 'the karma of the Pure Land' from the introductory chapter of *Kyogyoshinsho* turns up; the line 'the aspiration for birth in the Pure Land' (*ganshojodo*). To walk the Buddha way of the aspiration is exactly what our religion wants.

In other words the *dobokai* movement takes as its point of departure an analysis of the present day, and from there it starts in the Mahayana-bodhisattva way with great seriousness. That is why *dobokai* becomes a place to listen to the teachings of the law (*dharma*), together with the sangha practising *nembutsu*. We shall join the pathway of our forefathers.

To carry out activities in the *dobokai* movement in the right way we shall from this year study the leaflet called 'Manual for Propagators', and thus go through the Propagators' course, parts one and two, which are one of the three pillars of the *dobokai* movement. After this the participants become *suishinbotai* (i.e. 'mothers of propagators'), who are in charge of the memorial day meetings (*gomeinichi no tsudoi*) in the various temples on the memorial day of the founder, Shinran Shonin, the 28th each month, and who strive (*negau*) to make the religious character of Shin Buddhism based on gratitude (*hoon*) alive in our generation.

ON SETTING UP COURSES FOR PROPAGATORS
MEMORIAL DAY MEETINGS AND THE RELIGIOUS CHARACTER
OF SHIN BUDDHISM

The teaching of *hongannembutsu*, which the Founder, Shinran Shonin, expounded, has penetrated the lives of the individual believers and has naturally given shape to customs and traditions. As Rennyo Shonin said: 'First of all it is right and fitting to be sincerely grateful for our salvation on this memorial day (*gomeinichi*).' Thus it is an important part of the background of the religious character of Shin Buddhism that the Founder Shinran Shonin's memorial day meeting is held at all temples on the 28th in each month. For the individual believer, this meeting is of highest importance. There is a long tradition, in fact, to hear the law (*dharma*) on this occasion as a question of life and death; the individual believer at this point ought to grasp his firm belief in the reality of the true vow and to let himself be embraced by the good karma. It is a fact that if we should not be blessed with good karma, our birth in the Pure Land would become insecure and dwindle, and our destiny would become full of grief and woe. By hearing the law, the *nembutsu*-person experiences a drastic birth which opens up for joy by finding the meaning of life. As Akao no Doshu (from Toyama-ken, Higashi Tonami-gun) said: 'Say your morning service (*tsutome*) regularly. Once a month go to the local temple to get instruction. Go once a year to the main temple (*gohonji*).' In this way the *nembutsu*-person as a witness of truth has a practical life-style. This life-style reveals the character of Shin Buddhism which is intimately connected with family life and the local environment.

But the characteristics of Shin Buddhism have disappeared with the increasing lack of contact between family members, the pluralism of the family structure and the dominion that material culture has over spiritual culture given the conditions of modern life.

We lead a rational and pleasant life. But are we not in this way locked in by our private sympathies, pressed into spiritual isolation and exposed to unspeakable unrest and pain? Here the true concern of religion ought to show itself; but religion today has become the celebration of festivals and prayers for success – it has become more and more engulfed by increasing secularization.

But in such a situation it is in reality possible to start in earnest to seek the meaning of life. As Rennyo Shonin said: 'It is at all times possible to convert our evil and erring minds, to believe from this moment and turn to the 'other power' (*tariki*) of the true vow.' He recommends that we each month meet on Shinran's memorial day and by listening to the law turn our minds to the true teaching.

When we initiate the *dobokai* movement anew, it is really this that we want and pray for.

4 Shin Buddhism and the Arts and Crafts

What is religious art?

According to Richard B. Pilgrim in *Buddhism and the Arts of Japan*:

> 'It might be useful to think of religious art as that type of religious expression which representationally symbolizes, presentationally embodies, and performatively transforms varying life situations within the context of an understanding of sacrality and by use of aesthetic form (visual, performing and literary arts). Such a way of 'defining' religious art allows us to treat and distinguish the religious functions of art while at the same time discussing the arts themselves. To overlook these functions would be to miss the *Buddhism* in the art, or to risk seeing the arts as merely decorative appendages to what just happens to be a religion.'

With this in mind we can turn to some of the art forms in Shin Buddhism.

Among the literary arts Shandao's 'Parable of the White Path', one of the best known popular texts of Pure Land Buddhism, will do for a start. It was commented on by Shinran himself in *Kyogyoshinsho*. Its popularity is also seen from the fact that there are numerous illustrations of the white path, some of them are hanging silk scrolls dating back to the Kamakura period. The one introduced in this book is taken from an inexpensive manual meant for Shin followers and sold in one of the many shops with religious paraphernalia in the Honganji-district of Kyoto. Illustrations the size of posters are also to be found in Shin temples.

However, visual arts are not as important in Shin Buddhism as in, for instance, Shingon Buddhism with its many-coloured mandalas. There are Pure Land mandalas such as the *Taima mandala*, based on the *Sutra on Contemplation of Amitayus (Amida)*, one of the three basic Pure Land sutras, but they are not Shin. Mandalas are for visualization and meditation, and these are not Shin practices. In the words of Rennyo (1414-99), the second founder of Shin Buddhism:

> In other schools, pictorial representations are valued more than Buddha-name recitation images, and statues of wood are valued more than paintings. But in our tradition, painting is revered more than sculpture and images of the invocation of the Buddha's name are revered more than paintings.

Characters of Namu-amida-butsu: ① *(Nishi Honganji) and* ② *(Higashi Honganji) are by Shinran,* ③ *(Gasenji) and* ④ *(Keisenji) are by Rennyo*

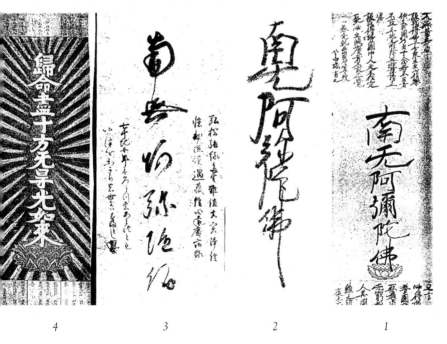

4   3   2   1

Shinran himself is also said to have rejected traditional *raigo* images (paintings of the descent of Amida Buddha to bring believers to the Pure Land) and representations in sculpture and painting of the Buddhas and bodhisattvas. This helps to explain why types of painting called *komyo honzon* ('ray-emitting devotional object') with nine- and six-character invocations (*Namu Amida Butsu*) were the main devotional images from earliest times. Shinran wrote such invocations on scrolls as objects of worship at the request of followers, not so that they implied any merit to the follower, as in the general Buddhist tradition, but as a reflection of the bond between Shinran and his followers. The originals still exist.

Nevertheless, there was a need for Shin followers to stimulate their visual abilities, and we know that portraits of Shinran, like the *Anjo no goei* and *Kagami no goei* from the Kamakura period and now at Nishi Hongan-ji, Kyoto, served that purpose. So did also the illustrations to Shinran's biography, *Godensho* (see Text 2 in this book). The illustrations reproduced here are modern and from a popular edition used at Ho-onko at Higashi Hongan-ji, but such *Den'e* pictures go back to the time of Kakunyo (1270-1351), Shinran's great-grandson.

However, it is to the literary arts we must turn to find the strongest influences of Shin Buddhism on the arts.

Kamo no Chomei's classic *The Ten Foot Square Hut* should be mentioned, though not influenced by Shin Buddhism but by Pure Land thought in general. Kamo no Chomei (1153-1216) lived at the same turbulent time as Shinran.

In *haiku* poetry Basho (1644-94) is a Zen Buddhist and intellectual, but Issa Kobayashi (1763-1827) is Shin and appeals to the feelings, to Shin followers. (Likewise some Shin interpreters maintain – though no art historian will probably agree with them – that in the field *ukiyo-e*, coloured woodprints, Hokusai is Zen, and Hiroshige is Shin. And some gardens like Kinkakuji – The Golden Pavilion – to these Shin interpreters is Zen, whereas Ginkakuji – The Silver Pavilion – is Shin.)

About *noh* plays experts disagree, but one Western authority, Arthur Waley, believes they are Shin influenced. Others, like Royall Tyler, think it impossible to distinguish between Shin and Zen and find the discussion 'unimportant beside the legacy of an older, richly complex Buddhism that embraced, more or less closely, nearly every concept of the sacred held in Japan'.

One special group of people, the *myokonin*, deserve special

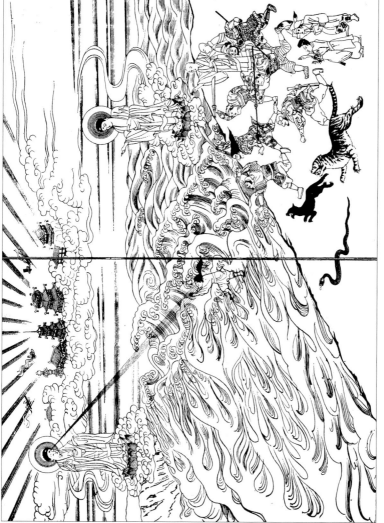

Parable of the White Path: from a Higashi Honganji leaflet

mention. To Daisetz Suzuki they were the quintessence of Shin Buddhism. The name means 'wondrous, happy people' and they were simple, unlearned people, often craftsmen and peasants, who wrote ecstatic verse about their devotion to Amida. Saichi Asahara (1850-1933) is a fine example.

In the folk crafts movement (*mingei*) the leading proponent, Yanagi Soetsu (1889-1961) himself used Shin Buddhist concepts to explain his aesthetic. Closely allied to the movement, Munakata Shiko (1903-75), the famous woodblock artist, worked in a Shin Buddhist environment and often took motifs from Buddhism.

Naturally, some modern novelists like Niwa Fumio (b. 1904) have been influenced by Shin, being brought up in a Shin Buddhist temple.

In many books on Japan arts are almost monopolized by Zen Buddhism. To Shin Buddhists this is a qualified truth.

Text 20

Shandao: *Parable of the White Path*

*S*handao (613-681) *is the fifth patriarch in Shin Buddhism. Shinran listed 7 patriarchs in all (see Text 5): two from India (Nagarjuna and Vasubandu), three from China (Tanluan, Daochuo and Shandao) and two from Japan (Genshin and Honen).*

'The Parable of the White Path' is one of the most popular literary texts in Shin Buddhism. Illustrations, like the one in this book, often decorate the walls of Shin temples and text and illustration can be bought in inexpensive books for lay people.

Shinran brought 'The Parable of the White Path' in his main theological work, Kyogyoshinsho, a systematized collection of valuable texts in Shin Buddhism, together with his own commentary.

S uppose there is a traveller journeying one hundred thousand li towards the west, when suddenly, along the way, he comes upon two rivers [in a single channel] – one of fire, extending south, and one of water, extending north. Each river is one hundred paces across, immeasurably deep, and endless to the north and south. Dividing the fire and water is a single white path four or five inches wide. This path, from the eastern bank to the western bank, is one hundred paces in length. Billows of water surge over the path and flames sweep up to scorch it. Water and fire thus alternate without break.

Now the traveller has already gone far into the vast and solitary wilderness; there is no one to be seen. But bands of brigands and wild beasts lurk there, and seeing the traveller alone, they vie with each other to kill him. Fearing for his life, the traveller at once flees towards the west, when without warning the great river appears. He reflects: 'I can see no end to this river either to the north or south. In the middle is a white path, but it is exceedingly narrow. Although the two banks are but slightly separated, how is it possible to cross? Assuredly this day I shall die. If I turn back, brigands and wild beasts will press closer and closer upon me. If I run north or south, beasts and poisonous insects will contend with each other to attack me. If I venture on the path westward, surely I will plunge into the two currents of water and fire.'

There are no words to express the terror and despair that fill him at this point. He thinks further to himself: 'If I turn back now, I die. If I remain here, I die. If I go forward, I die. There is no way for me to escape death. Therefore, I choose to go forth, venturing on this path. Since this path exists, it must be possible to cross the rivers.'

When this thought occurs to him, he suddenly hears an encouraging voice of someone on the eastern bank: 'O traveller, just resolve to follow the path forward! You will certainly not encounter the grief of death. But if you stay where you are, you will surely die.'

Further, someone on the western bank calls out to him: 'O traveller, with mind that is single, with right-mindedness, come at once! I will protect you. Have no fear of plunging to grief in the water or fire.' The traveller, having heard the exhortation on his side of the river and the call from the other, immediately acquires firm resolution in body and mind and decisively takes the path, advancing directly without entertaining any doubt or apprehension.

When he has gone one or two paces, the brigands on the eastern bank call out to him: 'O traveller, come back! This path is treacherous and permits no crossing. You are certain to meet death. None of us address you thus with evil intent.'

The traveller hears the voices calling him, but he gives no backward glance. Thinking only of the path, he advances directly forward with mind that is single, forthwith reaches the western side, and is free forever of all afflictions. He meets his good friend, and his joy is boundless. This is the parable.

□

Now to apply the parable: *The eastern bank* is the burning house, that is this saha world. *The western bank:* the precious land of perfect bliss. *The brigands and wild beasts calling with treacherous familiarity:* a sentient being's six sense organs, the six forms of perception, the six kinds of objects, the five aggregates, and the four elements. *The wilderness where no one is to be seen:* one constantly joins with evil companions, without ever meeting a true teacher. *The two currents of water and fire:* sentient beings' greed and desire are likened to water, their anger and hatred to fire. *The white path in the middle four or five inches wide:* amidst sentient beings' blind passions of greed and anger, a pure mind that aspires for birth in the Pure Land is awakened. Since the greed and anger are intense, they are like the water and fire. Since the good mind is slight, it is like the white path. Further, *billows of water constantly surge over the path:* desires arise incessantly to defile the good mind. *Flames ceaselessly scorch the path:* anger and hatred consume the dharma-treasure of virtue. *The traveller follows the path and advances directly westward:* turning away from all practices, he advances directly westward. *He hears a voice of someone on the eastern bank encouraging him and exhorting him, and following the path, advances directly westward:* Śākyamuni has already entered nirvana and people of later times cannot meet him. His teachings still remain, however, and we can follow them. They are like that voice. *When he has gone one or two paces, the brigands call him back:* people of different understandings, different practices or false views, with their own misguided opinions, one after another seek to confuse him, claiming that he will commit evil and fail. *Someone on the western bank calls to him:* this is the intent of Amida's Vow. *The traveller forthwith reaches the western side; he meets his good friend, and his joy is boundless:* sentient beings long sinking in birth-and-death and for innumerable kalpas lost in transmigration, being bound in delusion by their own karma, have no means of gaining emancipation for themselves. Reverently embracing Śākyamuni's teaching in his exhortations to advance westward and obeying Amida's call to us with his compassionate heart, the traveller accepts and accords with the mind of the two honoured ones; never giving a thought to the two rivers of water and fire and taking the call of the honoured ones to heart at every moment, he entrusts himself to the path of the power of the Vow. After his death, he attains birth in that land and meets the Buddha. How boundless is his joy!

Ueda & Hirota: *Shinran – an Introduction*
to His Thought (Hongwanji International Center
1989), pp. 291-294.

Text 21

Kamo no Chomei: *From 'The Ten Foot Square Hut'*

*K*amo no Chomei (1156?-1216) came to typify the literary recluse when, after having been denied a hereditary post at the Kamo Shrines in Kyoto, he secluded himself in the mountains around Kyoto, first at Ohara, later at Uji. His famous book, Hojoki ('The Ten Foot Square Hut') is a good example of Pure Land piety in medieval Japan.

Ceaselessly the river flows, and yet the water is never the same, while in the still pools the shifting foam gathers and is gone, never staying for a moment. So is man and his habitation.

In the stately ways of our shining Capital the dwellings of high and low raise their roofs in rivalry as in the beginning, but few indeed there are that have stood for many generations. This year falling into decay and the next built up again, how often does the mansion of one age turn into the cottages of the next. And so, too, are they who live in them. The streets of the city are thronged as of old, but of the many people we meet there how very few are those that we knew in our youth. Dead in the morning and born at night, so man goes on for ever, unenduring as the foam on the water.

□

I do not say these things from envy of rich people, but only from comparison of my early days with the life I live now.

Since I forsook the world and broke off all its ties, I have felt neither fear nor resentment. I commit my life to fate without special wish to live or desire to die. Like a drifting cloud I rely on none and have no attachments. My only luxury is a sound sleep and all I look forward to is the beauty of the changing seasons.

Now the Three Phenomenal Worlds, the World of Desire, the World of Form, and the World of No-form, are entirely of the mind. If the mind is not at rest, horses and oxen and the Seven Precious Things and Palaces and Pavilions are of no use. With this lonely cottage of mine, this hut of one room, I am quite content. If I go out to the Capital I may feel shame at looking like a mendicant priest, but when I come back home here I feel compassion for those who are still bound by the attraction of earthly things. If any doubt me let them consider the fish. They do not get tired of the water; but if you are not a fish you cannot understand their feelings. Birds, too, love the woods, but unless you are yourself a bird you cannot know how they feel. It is just so with the life of a hermit: How can you understand unless you experience it?

Now the moon of my life has reached its last phase and my remaining years draw near to their close. When I soon approach the Three Ways of the Hereafter what shall I have to regret? The Law of Buddha teaches that we should shun all clinging to the world of phenomena, so that the affection I have for this thatched hut is in some sort a sin, and my attachment to this solitary life may be a hindrance to enlightenment. Thus I have been babbling, it may be, of useless pleasures, and spending my precious hours in vain.

In the still hours of the dawn I think of these things, and to myself I put these questions: 'Thus to forsake the world and dwell in the woods, has it been to discipline my mind and practise the Law of Buddha or not? Have I put on the form of a recluse while yet my heart has remained impure? Is my dwelling but a poor imitation of that of Saint Vimalakirrti while my merit is not even equal to that of Suddhipanthaka the most stupid of the followers of Buddha? Is this poverty of mine but the retribution for the offences of a past existence, and do the desires of an impure heart still arise to hinder my enlightenment? And in my heart there is no answer. The most I can do is to murmur two or three times a perchance unavailing invocation to Buddha.'

The last day of the third month of the second year of the era of Kenryaku. By me the Sramana Ren-in in my hut on Toyama Hill.

Sad am I at heart
When the moon's bright silver orb
Sinks behind the hill.

But how blest 't will be to see
Amida's perpetual light.

(*The Ten Foot Square Hut and Tales of the Heike*,
tr. by A.L. Sadler (Tuttle 1990)(orig. 1928), p. 1, 19-21)

Text 22

Issa Kobayashi:
From 'The Year of My Life'

Issa Kobayashi (1763-1827), the haiku poet, wrote Oraga Haru (1820), 'The Year of My Life', on the birth and death of his second child. After marrying a much younger woman in 1814, four children were born in quick succession, but none of them lived long.

The poetic form is that of haiban, haiku *mixed with prose.*

Those who insist on salvation by faith and devote their minds to nothing else are bound all the more firmly by their singlemindedness, and fall into the hell of attachment of their own salvation. Again, those who are passive and stand to one side waiting to be saved, consider that they are already perfect and rely rather on Buddha than on themselves to purify their hearts – these, too, have failed to find the secret of genuine salvation. The question then remains – how do we find it? But the answer, fortunately, is not difficult.

We should do far better to put this vexing problem of salvation out of our minds altogether and place our reliance neither on faith nor on personal virtue, but surrender ourselves completely to the will of Buddha. Let him do as he will with us – be it to carry us to heaven, or to hell. Herein lies the secret.

Once we have determined on this course, we need care nothing for ourselves. We need no longer ape the busy spider by stretching the web of our desire across the earth, nor emulate the greedy farmer by taking extra water into our own fields at the expense of our neighbours. Moreover, since our minds will be at peace, we need not always be saying our prayers with hollow voice, for we shall be entirely under the benevolent direction of Buddha.

This is the salvation – this is the peace of mind we teach in our religion. Blessed be the name of Buddha.

Tomo-kaku-mo anata makase no toshi no kure
   In any case
Leaving all to you
   Now, at the end of the year.

(Issa, *Oragu Haru*, tr. by
Nobuyuki Yuasa (University of
California Press, 1960), p. 139-40)

Text 23

Issa Kobayashi: *From 'The Seventh Journal'*

Issa Kobayashi (1763-1827) spent many years on journeys on foot writing poems along the way. His style is down-to-earth, full of animal images. The form is haibun.

I made a pilgrimage to the temple of Tōkaiji in Fuse. Feeling sorry for the chickens that followed after me longingly, I bought some rice from a house in front of the temple gate and scattered it among the violets and dandelions. Soon they began to fight among themselves here and there. Meanwhile, pigeons and sparrows came flying down from the boughs and were quietly eating up the rice. The chickens coming back, they flew off to the branches again, sooner than they wanted, no doubt wishing that the kicking match had lasted longer. Samurai, farmers, artizans, merchants and all the rest are just like this in the way they live.

   Scattering rice, –
This also is a sin,
   The fowls kicking one another!

(Blyth, *Haiku* Vol. 1
(Hokuseido Press, 1981),
p. 303-304)

Text 24

Issa Kobayashi: *Haiku*

The first of the three haiku *poems is the best known of all of Issa's* haiku *poems written upon the death of his idolized daughter, the third of his children to die in infancy.*

Haiku are an original Japanese poetic form consisting of three lines of five, seven and five syllables respectively. They are most often used to give a instantaneous, impressionistic image.

The world of dew –
A world of dew it is indeed,
And yet, and yet . . .

A blessing indeed –
This snow on the bed-quilt,
This, too, from the Pure Land.

The Nightingale!
In His Highness's presence chamber
It is the same song!

(*The Autumn Wind*, tr. by Lewis Mackenzie
(Kodansha 1990), p. 5, 7, 90)

Text 25

Saichi Asahara: *Poems of a myokonin*

Saichi Asahara (1850-1933) was a builder of ships and later a clog-maker. He wrote his poems on wooden shavings without any regard for poetic form. His art is totally artless.

A myokonin *is a lay practitioner of Shin Buddhism with profound experiential understanding of the workings of Amida. D.T. Suzuki (see Text 13), among others, has emphasized their importance in Japanese religious history. He collected the poems of Saichi Asahara towards the end of his life.*

a) I receive Amida San from Amida San,
   He has me say, 'Namu-Amida-Butsu'.

b) Compassion is Amida San.
   Compassion that makes me worship,
   'Namu-Amida-Butsu',
   Is 'Namu-Amida-Butsu'.

c) Great Favour
   That makes my sin a virtuous Buddha,
   'Namu-Amida-Butsu'.

d) Great favour, great favour, oh, great favour,
   This Buddha is the Buddha
   Who makes Saichi Buddha,
   The great favour that says 'Namu-Amida-Butsu'.

e) Namu Buddha is Saichi, Saichi is the Buddha.
   Saichi's satori comes, 'Namu-Amida-Butsu' –
   This is received, 'Namu-Amida-Butsu'.

(D.T. Suzuki: *Japanese Spirituality*, tr. by
Norman Waddell (Japan Society for the
promotion of Science 1972), pp. 182-83.)

Text 26

Yanagi Soetsu: *The Dharma Gate of Beauty – Shin Aesthetics*

Yanagi Soetsu (1889-1961) was a leading theorist of Japanese arts and crafts which he conveyed to the West. Early in his life he met the English ceramist Bernard Leach, with whom he formed a lifelong friendship. He travelled widely and wrote prolifically. He sought out anonymous craftsmen throughout Japan, and his collection of folkcrafts became the nucleus of the Japan Folkcraft Museum in Tokyo of which he was one of the founders in 1936.

Ido Tea-Bowl, from Yanagi: The Unknown Craftsman

When I come to attain Buddhahood, unless all the beings throughout my land are of one form and colour, unless there is no beauty and ugliness among them, I will not attain highest enlightenment.

THE LARGER SUTRA OF ETERNAL LIFE

In this fourth of Amida's forty-eight great vows are found words which can give us the basis upon which to erect an aesthetic.[1] Amida's declaration means that in the land of the Buddha the duality of beauty and ugliness does not exist.

As it is recorded that the Buddha did attain highest enlightenment, that the conditions in his vow stand fulfilled is unquestioned. In things' ultimate nature there are no dualities whatever. All things, in respect to their Buddha-nature, are of a purity that transcends relative oppositions such as beauty and ugliness. In the light of this original being dualism vanishes. For that reason it is sometimes described as 'the essential part', 'without birth-and-death', 'pure and undefiled from the very beginning'. It is also said to be 'stillness' or 'emptiness', to be 'originally not a single thing', or 'nothingness'. Not merely nothingness which holds onesidedly to nothingness, but nothingness which transcends the duality of nothingness and being. If this realm is not entered and made our own, then nothing is true.

The land of the Buddha is a land of supreme existence, not so

---

1 Briefly stated, the forty-eight vows of Amida Buddha, which appear in the *Larger Sutra of Eternal Life*, are variations of one basic vow: to save sentient beings from suffering by leading them out of their illusion to the Pure Land or Enlightenment, achieved in the practice of the Nembutsu. *Ed.*

much as a hint of beauty or ugliness is to be found in any corner of it. This same absoluteness is what sustains the original nature in us as well. No dualisms figure in our original nature either. For us, to dwell in form which is no form is our true form. The forms of beauty and ugliness are but the provisional semblances of reality.

Where then does this 'Dharma-gate' of beauty take us? What is it trying to teach and transmit to us? It says that dwelling in the inborn nature which transcends the duality of beauty and ugliness is to dwell in a condition of salvation, and this is true for whoever or whatever it may be. It tells us that as salvation is already promised, we should not immerse ourselves in profitless disputes over beauty and ugliness. Furthermore, it does not even ask that we be qualified to receive this salvation (how could faulted human beings possibly have such faultless qualifications?), for the Buddha is ready to welcome us into his land, having fulfilled all qualifications for us.

It teaches also that since salvation has been readied for us in this way, it would be inexcusable if we did not avail ourselves of it. Return to your intrinsic Buddha-nature which is beyond beauty and ugliness, apart from it there is no real or true beauty. This is what the religion of beauty teaches us.

☐

As I have said before, by their own power those of sufficient ability may eventually reach their goal. Their practice, based on the model of the Buddha's own wisdom, has from ancient times been carried through to completion by a few select monks. But what of the rest of mankind beyond number, incapable of saving themselves? It is their plight, falling under the Buddha's gaze, that arouses his compassion. Without the vow which issues from this compassion the salvation of ordinary men and women would be hopeless. He vows to save them because they are unable to save themselves. It is not too much to say that the compassion representing the fulfilment of his attainment of highest enlightenment was solely for the cause of such people.

That is why Shinran was brought to declare that the true object of his teaching was the evil man. That is an extremely audacious notion. At first it is difficult to comprehend. But if only we remember the depth of the Buddha's compassion, there can be no room for any doubt regarding its truth.

Involvement in discussions of talent or lack of talent comes to have little real importance in view of the way definitely promised by which even a talentless person can be saved just as he is. There is no overlooking the fact that many exceptional works of art have been made by nameless and illiterate craftsmen. Those Ido tea-bowls so highly praised by the great Tea masters are the best possible illustrations. We do not know the people who made them, but they were not the work of only one potter, or even several. Whoever they were they could only have been poor artisans. We can hardly suppose that each one of them was a man of genius. They were workmen of the most ordinary kind. They were making low-priced articles. They certainly were not giving any thought to making each piece beautiful. They threw them off simply and effortlessly. If the bowls are described as graceful, that was surely not sought by their makers. The bowls were allowed to follow their own ways into existence, naturally and inevitably. This accounts for the air of elegance with which they are so richly endowed. They are works untroubled by either beauty or ugliness, fashioned and appearing before the illness of illusion and doubt could arise. This freedom was gained precisely by virtue of their ordinariness and low cost. It is not something which could have been brought about by any ability in the artisans. The overall environment, the received traditions, the selfless work, the simple way of life, the natural materials and unsophisticated techniques, all combined in the flowering of these bowls. When those Korean potters were making their wares they were merely doing matter of factly what was expected of them. Is that not the reason the bowls were saved? It seems to me that here a common ground forms naturally with the teaching of Self-power and its ideal of 'everydayness'. That is why the Ido bowls, though the outcome or work of the Other-power, are found to suit the tastes of Zen. Here one cannot help feeling the oneness of the Self-power and Other-power schools.

Let me add one further point. Has any genius in later times been able to produce works to surpass the Ido tea-bowls fashioned so effortlessly by those ordinary men? It would seem extremely doubtful. To paraphrase Shinran's words from the *Tannishō* quoted a few pages ago: 'The genius can produce exceptional work, all the more so can the common man – with the help of the Buddha.'

(*Eastern Buddhist*, Vol. XII, No.2
(October 1979), p. 5-6, 15-16)

Text 27

'Doshu of Akao' – a woodblock print by Munakata Shiko

Munakata Shiko (1903-75) was the leading woodblock artist of his time with no less than three museums in Japan named after him. Munakata is considered heavily influenced by Jodoshinshu and the folk arts movement, as the following quotation shows: 'The essence of *hanga* (woodcuts) lies in the fact that one must give in to the ways of the board. There is a power in the board, and one cannot force the tool against the power. It is this power which lies outside the artist, rather than any power which lies within him, that dominates the creation of *hanga*.'

Woodblock print by Monakata Shiko: Doshu of Akao – 'original'

When he made the woodblock print, he was inspired by a small wood-carving with the same motif: Doshu of Akao.

Doshu of Akao (d.1516) was a disciple of Rennyo and by Daisetz Suzuki described as 'heading the list of the myokonin' (see Text 25). He is depicted sleeping on 48 sticks of split firewood, corresponding to Amida's 48 vows, and the story behind the wood carving and the woodblock print is as follows:

Doshu had many scars that he always tried to hide from other people. When a neighbour, overcome with curiosity, peeked in to see what Doshu was doing at bedtime, he discovered that Doshu slept on top of the 48 sticks with only a thin quilt over himself. He would say the *nenbutsu* every time he turned over.

The man later went to Doshu and said, 'You always tell us that we will be saved just by entrusting ourselves to Amida Buddha, but there's more to it, isn't there? Really, we have to do that difficult kind of practice to be saved, don't we ?' 'Not at all,' replied Doshu. 'There's no more to it than what I said. But if a stubborn fellow like me sleeps on top of bedding, he'd sleep the whole night through, completely unaware of the Buddha's benevolence. By making it difficult to sleep, I'm at least able to think of the Tathagata's compassion when I wake and say the nembutsu.'

The characters in the upper right-hand corner of the woodcut constitute the first of Doshu's 21 rules: 'As long as life lasts, never forget the most important matter: the afterlife.'

Text 28

Niwa Fumio: *A Child's Ho-onko*

Niwa Fumio (b. 1904) succeeded his father as a Shin priest but left the family temple in 1932 to become a writer. His works are collected in 28 volumes and he is considered an important novelist. He draws heavily on his Shin Buddhist background.

Note: Scrolls similar to the ones mentioned in the text can be seen at Text 2.

The autumn services in commemoration of St Shinran were the most spectacular event of the year at Butsuoji, as at Senshuji and all the other temples of the sect. Many preparations had to be made before the services began. The yellow and purple curtains were hung up again at the head of the temple steps and in front of the porch of the house, and rows of paper lanterns set up in the courtyard, the whole compound taking on a festival air. Ryokun always enjoyed those services. With a feeling of excited anticipation he would stare up at the purple curtain which hung low over the door of the house, darkening the hall inside, and at the ornaments and decorations in the temple itself. The shrine was resplendent with the newly-polished Five Ornaments and oil-lamps; the gilded pillars seemed to shine for the occasion with a mysterious brilliancy. Treading softly on the mats so as to make no noise, Ryokun inspected the shrine and the recess behind it and on either side. Every year he would spend hours staring at the eight scrolls hung in the *tokonoma* of the recess. For most of the year there were only four – one pair consisting only of Chinese characters, the other of a number of portraits of saints, whose names Ryokun did not know – they included the 'Seven Patriarchs' of the Pure Land sect, Ryuju Bosatsu, Tenshin Bosatsu, Unran Daishi, Doshaku Zenji, Zendo Daishi, Genshin Sozu, and Honen Shonin. The scrolls were old and faded, so that it was no longer easy to distinguish the faces. Before the autumn services, however, they were taken down and replaced with eight scrolls depicting the life of Shinran.

The first of the many scrolls dealing with events in the saint's life was painted by Joga of Korakuji, with a commentary by Kakunyo, in the 30th year of Einin, only thirty-five years after the saint's death. The Butsuoji scrolls were copied from those preserved at Senshuji, which are generally considered to be the finest extant.

There was no one else in the hall. Ryokun stood looking up at the scrolls, absorbed in the painted scenes; the *tokonoma* shelves above which the scrolls were hung were unusually high, about the level of his chest. The first of the four scenes on the first scroll showed the saint receiving his first tonsure as a Buddhist priest, at Seiren Temple in Awataguchi. Above the painting ran the commentary: 'Inspired by a longing to spread the Law, and aided by the merit of a former existence, at the age of nine he visited the temple of his uncle, the former Chief Abbot Noritsuna, Lord of the third class of the second rank, where he received the tonsure and was given the name of Noriyasu.' Ryokun was fascinated by the details of the scene – ceremonial carriages, the plum blossom, the retainers dragging unwilling oxen, the court pages, the big white tile-covered walls, the figures sitting so straight and stiff, looking as if at any moment they might topple over. Below the first painting was the description of the second: 'In the spring of the first year of Kennin, wishing to withdraw from the world, he visited the saint Honen at the Kissui Temple.' All the figures in this picture were priests. Much of the commentary was too difficult for Ryokun to read; but the sequence of pictures was enough to give him a general idea of the story, and he enjoyed working it out for himself.

Of the saint's birth and childhood nothing is known for certain. Tradition has it that he was born in the village of Hino near Kyoto on 1 April in the third year of Shoan, in the reign of the Emperor Takakura, the son of the Lord of Fujiwara Arinori, Chief Lord-in-Waiting to the Dowager Empress, and Yoshimitsu, daughter of Minamoto Yoshinobu; and that as a child he was called Matsuwakamaru. But there is no historical evidence for this story, which may have been invented for their own purposes by the priests of the Honganji Temple when they were faced with the necessity, thirty-five years after the saint's death, of compiling an 'official' biography.

No such doubts troubled Ryokun, as he followed the narrative from one picture to the next, the dramatic representation of incidents in the saint's life making them live in his imagination far more than any reading of the archaic script of the commentary could have done. Most of all he was thrilled by the picture of Ben'en, the notorious leader of the mountain hermits of the Hitachi region, attempting to kill the saint on Mt Itajiki. Clad in heavy armour from head to foot, with a halberd in one hand and a bow in the other, and a look of fiendish hatred on his face, the hermit lay in wait for his victim, who was building himself a cell in a field. 'A certain hermit,' the commentary began, 'felt spite against the Law, and harbouring evil in his heart, sought out the saint in the mountain. Many times he lay in wait for him hoping to strike him down on one of his journeys to the solitude of Mt Itajiki; but always he failed of his purpose. Indeed, if we think deeply, it seems no less than a miracle that the saint did not fall into his hands. . . . At last he determined he would visit the saint openly. When he reached his cell, the saint at once came out to meet him. The moment the hermit saw his gracious countenance, all malice vanished from his heart; he wept in sorrowful repentance. Nor did the saint show any trace of fear at his confession of the dark purpose that had filled his mind. Casting away his sword and breaking his bow in two, the hermit straightway abandoned his hermit's robe and cowl, and returning to the fold of the true Law, attained to the salvation for which he longed. . . .'

The scrolls were as exciting as a popular novel in the drama and variety of the events they depicted, so that inability to read the commentaries in no way lessened Ryokun's enjoyment of them. The last picture of all, though, was frightening; it always made him wish he had never looked at the scrolls at all, it was so dark and sad. In the right-hand corner, seven or eight priests were carrying a bier on poles, the leader holding a pine-torch above his head. The body of Shinran lay stretched on the bier. Huge pine-trees and mountain precipices dwarfed the little procession as it made its way to the pyre on the opposite side of the picture, where enormous red tongues of flame leapt forward to meet the bier and its burden. Three more priests, shoulders bared and robes tucked up above their knees, were stirring the fire with long iron poles. In the shadow of a crag nearby four or five other priests stood with linked hands. Ryokun hated them – it struck him there was something brutal, even murderous, in their posture and expression, as if they were gloating over the burning of the body of the saint instead of mourning for him. No less gruesome in this final picture were two other figures, white-hooded after the manner of mountain hermits, who were emerging from the forest on the left of the picture, above the pyre. Finally, half-hidden behind its surrounding fence, there was the open, waiting tomb.

(*The Buddha Tree* (Tuttle, 1989),
p. 193-95)

5 Rituals in Shin Buddhist temples – notably Higashi Honganji

The head temple in Shinshu Otaniha, Higashi Honganji, is impressive in size. The present buildings were erected in 1895 after a fire. The plan shows that there are many buildings besides the main buildings, the Founder's Hall and Amida's Hall, and many activities take place (see Chapter 3). Here, close to 9,000 temples from 30 district offices, more than 16,000 priests (of these 1750 women) and about 5.5 million Japanese seek guidance. To this must be added three overseas areas: North America, Hawai'i and South America, where a Shin Buddhist Mission has been carried out in the wake of Japanese immigration.

On a normal day the grounds look very large although there is a steady number of tourists and followers who visit the temple. They usually start with the Founder's Hall, stop in the corridor between that and Amida's Hall, and end their visit in Amida's Hall. The stop in the corridor is in front of a glass case with the 'hair rope'. When the new buildings were being erected in 1895, difficulties arose due to the weight of the timbers being used. Conventional ropes were not strong enough, but when word of the difficulties reached local temples throughout Japan, female believers cut off their hair to make massive hair ropes that were capable of lifting the timbers, so the brochure tells the visitor.

When the annual Ho-onko takes place the buildings are full. Ho-onko means 'a gathering to repay favours'. *On* and *hoon* are usually thought of as Confucian concepts, but they are very much used in Shin Buddhism, too. The debt to pay back is the debt to

The two main temples at Higashi Honganji

Imperial Entrance at Higashi Honganji

Aerial view of Higashi Honganji

Shinran, and the keynote of the memorial festival is gratitude. At Ho-onko it is possible for the believers to get their Buddha name at a ceremony called *Kikyoshiki*. Ho-onko takes place at slightly different times in different temples although Shinran's death in Shinshu Otaniha is 28 November.

There are other events celebrated at Higashi Honganji, among these are the New Year ceremonies, *Shusho-e*, the first week of January, *O-Higan*, at spring and autumn equinoxes, the spring rituals, *Haru no hoyo*, the first four days of April, and *O-Bon* in July-August. *O-Higan* and *O-Bon* are collective rituals for the dead. Moreover, there are memorial ceremonies for Rennyo, the organizer and second founder of Shin Buddhism, on 25 March, and a corresponding ceremony for Prince Shotoku on 22 February. Finally, *Susu-harai* deserves mentioning: the annual cleaning of the temple when the believers beat the *tatami* with bamboo sticks, while others drive out the dust using huge fans – a very popular event.

The temple is also used by individual families who have memorial services for their dead carried out, for instance *Shumidan* ceremonies. (See description in Chapter 6.)

Religious life around local temples in towns and villages is different. The Shin Buddhist priest has the role of spiritual adviser to the congregation. Among other tasks he visits the elderly and is kept aware of the joyful and sorrowful events in individual families. The families have their memorial ceremonies carried out by the local priest, as well as the funeral services. Early each morning daily prayers are offered. The annual ceremonies are carried out as they are in the main temple, but on a smaller scale. Text 33 is a description of an intimate Ho-onko in a provincial town, Murakami in Niigata, which to Shin Buddhists is perhaps more genuine than the big one in Kyoto.

Text 29

Plan of Higashi Honganji

In Karasuma Dori, main street of Kyoto, not far from the central station, Higashi Honganji lies, huge and massive. There are remains of a moat around the temple as a reminder of the unruly time when monks and priests fought in the streets. The district around the temple is today full of shops which supply religious inventory to temples and private homes, for instance *butsudan*, the shelf or cabinet where the family puts up the memorial tablets (*ihai*) for their dead members and where small statues or prints of Amida are placed. There are also many small hotels and restaurants which cater for the thousands of followers who come to the annual ceremonies.

For ordinary visitors to the temple there are two gates: the biggest one opening up to the founder Shinran's temple (*Goeido*) and a smaller one facing Amida's temple (*Amidado*). The biggest gate has two storeys, and a room on the second storey with statues

Plan of Higashi Honganji

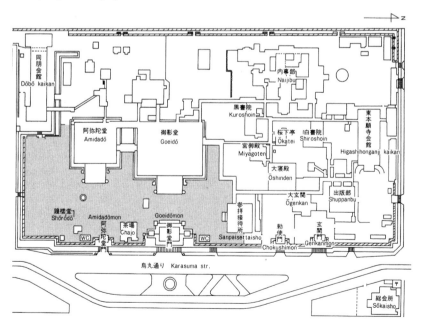

of Gautama Buddha, Maitreya (the future Buddha), and Ananda, one of the earliest disciples of Gautama Buddha. The scene is the one in which Buddha preaches 'The Larger Sutra of Eternal Life', (*Sukhavati-vyuha-sutra*), the most important sutra in Shin Buddhism. A third gate (*Chokushimon*) is the Imperial Envoy's gate which is only used by visitors from the Japanese imperial court. Finally, there is a locked gate (*Genkanmon*) leading to the administrative building. Today, people on an errand there use the gate in the northern side street, the same way as people visiting the headquarters of the Dobo-kai movement (*Dobo kaikan*) use the gate in the southern side street.

Tourists and ordinary visitors are only allowed in the cross-hatched part of the map above. In bad weather and cold they seek shelter in the tea-room (*Chajo*). There seems to be a fixed path where people start with the Founder's temple, walking to Amida's temple by the corridor past the hair rope and ending up in Amida's temple. Some of them make use of the small dragon fountain in the middle of the court to rinse their hands and mouths, the way it is also done at a Shinto shrine. Moreover, there is a bell tower (*Shorodo*) in the courtyard used only at annual events.

Believers who wish to have ceremonies performed go to the reception office (*Sanpaisettaisho*) where they are met by officiating priests. The administration of all of the Shinshu Otani sect is carried out from the administration offices (*Higashihonganji kaikan*) and the sect has its own publishing department in the building called *Shuppanbu*. Between the administration and the temples there are a number of state rooms with costly sliding doors, many of them presents from emperors. There is also a *noh* stage which is only shown to distinguished guests. This part of the temple grounds is used as a museum. Finally, in the north-western corner there is the private mansion of the Otani family (*Naijibu*), isolated from the rest of the temple.

It should be added that to the west of Higashi Honganji there is a comparable temple on Horikawa Street called Nishi (West) Honganji, head temple of the Jodo Shinshu Honganji branch of Shin Buddhism. The main structure is similar, but Nishi Honganji is older and has more important architectural and artistic features than Higashi Honganji. The split of the Honganji into two divisions came in the seventeenth century as a result of politics and dynastic rivalry. (See General Introduction.)

Text 30

Ho-onko at Higashi Honganji, November 1992 – a description

The lights are already hung out by the time I arrive at the temple at about 9.30 on the morning of the first day of the annual Ho-onko. There are also other signs of the approaching festival, for instance the stalls outside the temple are full of *juzu* (rosaries) which are used especially in popular Buddhist sects. No doubt there will be a good market during the coming week. Inside the gates there are also preparations going on. Various temporary buildings have been set up for catering to the pilgrims. In front of *Goeido* (Founder's Hall) and *Amidado* (Amida Hall) are huge cloths carrying the Higashi Honganji logo, slightly faded. But the halls themselves are closed until the ceremonial opening.

In one of the waiting-rooms, the *Chajo* (Tea room), the early arrivals can get a free cup of green tea. All the time a video is being shown about the Ho-onko.

Early next morning, Sunday at 6.30 am, I participate in the sutra chanting, *Jincho*. When I get to the temple grounds I see long lines of pilgrims walking from *Dobokaikan* to *Amidado* with the characteristic white scarves over their shoulders. The scarves bear the names of Higashi Honganji and Ho-onko, and they give a sense of togetherness. Later they become a prized souvenir. First they walk into *Amidado* for a short prayer, then *Goeido*. The temple priests come at the same time and the chanting begins with few pilgrims participating. They total about 400 in all. Besides the pilgrims with white scarves there are people with purple *kesa*, which is the small band symbolizing a priestly robe worn by priests off duty or some pious believers. There are no officials 'organizing' people who in general are behaving devoutly and using their discretion. Some converse and take photographs.

After 50 minutes' chanting most of the priests and about half the audience leave. It is time for *Ofumi howa*, letters by Rennyo followed by a sermon. It lasts about 20 minutes. Then it is time for the pilgrims to go back to the *Dobokaikan* while other spectators walk about the temple compound.

At 10.00 *Nicchu shue*, morning service, starts and now there are 8-10 buses parked outside the temple with more pilgrims – those who come for one day only. Many of the newly-arrived pass the dragon fountain in the middle of the court and perform *temizu*, purify themselves, in exactly the same way as one does at a Shinto shrine: pouring water over one's hands, while some drink from the thin jet of water with a wooden ladle. By now the sun is shining. Even though it is late November, it is like a European summer. The temples face east and take in the sunlight.

Inside *Goeido* the ceremony starts with a collection. Some pilgrims with baskets on long handles get up and weave their way through the audience. Almost everybody makes a donation, some in quite large notes.

The priests arrive and a bell is struck. What I have not noticed is a number of musicians who begin playing *gagaku*, ancient court music. (Afterwards, when I ask them about the origin of court music in a popular Buddhist sect, the people of the *shumusho*, the administration office, are not able to answer, but Shinshu Otaniha had strong connections with the Imperial household.) The music is antiphonal, a chorus of priests is supported by instruments; at times the music is in unison and very loud.

More people now, about 500, but also more unrest and less interest in the ceremony than in the morning. The ceremony does not really invite participation and only the inner core of the audience concentrate on what is taking place.

From time to time there is complete silence, then a priest's frail voice is heard and later all the priests and the musicians join together in a crescendo. But there is no officiating in front of the altar. Only the candles are replaced at intervals.

A bit restless, I glance at the wooden tablet above the altar with Shinran's honorary name given by the Meiji Emperor. *Kenshin Daishi*. 'Great Teacher who has revealed the Truth'. The aristocratic element in Shinshu Otaniha has the pride of place today.

About two hours later the morning service is over.

□

After lunch the temperature has risen again and there is a feeling of well-being in the temple grounds. The upper storey of *Goeidomon*, the main gate, is open for visitors. Here they see three statues: Shakyamuni, Ananda (one of the first disciples) and Maitreya, Buddha of the future. It is the situation in which Shakyamuni preaches the 'Larger Sutra of Eternal Life', the most important sutra in Pure Land Buddhism.

Assembly of believers, Ho-onko, 1992, Higashi Honganji

Believers cleaning the temple steps, Higashi Honganji

Over the loudspeakers a taped sermon is heard. It is a female preacher, a rarity. Later, there is some organ music in Western harmonization but the melody itself is unknown to me.

The pilgrims walk about the court – some in groups, some by themselves. I notice especially some women who have not only white scarves or bands, but are dressed all in white. They sweep and clean the grounds. Also the stone pavement at the gate was washed early in the morning.

During lunch various prayer meetings took place in the temple buildings behind the two main halls; there was also a prayer meeting for the office clerks from the administration building.

At two o'clock *Taiya shue*, the meeting on the eve of the anniversary of Shinran's death, begins. The money collectors walk down the rows of people. Another mite. The audience is smaller now. Only 2-300 and the number of priests exceeds 50. Among them is an important person in an orange surplice who is photographed by several people. He belongs to the Otani family, the chief priests. During the recitations, without music now, more people come.

I look at those closest to me. During the recitations one possibility is to pray. Two do that – without moving their lips, with closed eyes and the rosary between their fingers. One by one the beads pass through their fingers. At the same time there are people who come and go. Even whole groups of pilgrims do not join the service until now. Some are there for only 5-10 minutes. Here religious behaviour is allowed a great deal of latitude.

In front of me there are a couple of grandparents babysitting at the same time as participating in the annual big event in their temple. The grandchildren are 3-4 years old and they quarrel. *Obaasan*, the grandmother, has a job pacifying them, while *ojiisan*, the grandfather is concentrated and remote. At first sight he seems strict, but he smiles brightly when asked about something by the small girl. However, the children address the grandmother most and she has a store of chewing-gum and small toys.

There is nothing forbidding about the scene. People behave in various ways. Some hum together in unison with the priests' chanting, some relax and are lost in thought, still others are just curious and not involved – they are the ones who do not stay. Children and grown-ups are to be seen, but young parents are not as many as one should expect. It is taken for granted that there are periods in one's life when religion does not play any great role, especially in the case of young busy families. There is an equal distribution of the sexes and the old generations are by far the majority. It is obvious that the congregation is not well dressed and wealthy.

Apart from replacing the candles there are no changes in front of the altar. Recitations only. After one hour it is over, but a priest dressed in white comes in to sit down at a low table. Most of the participants have left the hall, and now also the priests with the high priest in orange in front. The pilgrims are advised by the young temple priests. The priest in white conducts *Ofumi howa*, the reading aloud of a letter by Rennyo and a sermon.

Finally, *Shoya*, the chanting of songs by Shinran. Small leaflets are handed out to those who do not have the texts. Especially *Shoshinge* is popular. This time most people participate.

At 5 pm the first full day of Hoonko is over and the gates close.

☐

(During the following week the scenery and the programme repeats itself. But when Wednesday comes the ceremonies reach their first culmination. Godensho, the biography of Shinran, is recited. It was written by Kakunyo (1270-1351), the great-grandson of Shinran.)

Today, Wednesday, there are more people in the Founder's Hall which is filled with more than 1,000 believers. The *Godensho* illustrations on the wall next to the altar have lit candles in front of them, and when the ceremony begins the big chandeliers in the ceiling are turned off. Slowly, slowly a small group of priests enter, carrying candles and a small chest. The atmosphere is one of darkness and sorrow. The most important priest sits down behind the chest, places the chest on a low table and the assistant priests leave. Then the chandeliers are lit again and I look around and see that many have brought small editions of the biography so that they can follow in the book.

The officiating priest takes off the lid of the chest in which the scrolls are hidden, and the first golden roll is opened, very slowly. It is the beginning of Shinran's life. The audience crane their necks and in a strong voice the priest begins the recitation. A single voice interprets the text ritually for one hour. Those who do not follow in their small books have bowed heads and some roll the beads in their rosaries. Today the women form the majority. It is six o'clock in the evening and many men are still at work.

The only variation is the pauses when the priest closes one roll and unbinds the next. Then the first priest reaches a crescendo, and the first half of the biography is over. He rises and is replaced by a younger priest with an incredible, penetrating voice. Too strained to be considered beautiful by Western standards, but very trained and technically adept.

We are near the end. One more crescendo and the strong voice brings us to the last part of Shinran's life.

When I leave it has grown dark and the splendid modern Kyoto Tower is reflected in the moat of the old temple. I am blinded by the neon lights of a *pachinko* pintable arcade. Strange contrasts.

□

(All through the week the believers have the possibility of getting their homyo, *which is the Buddha name they will be known by after their death. It is a ceremony which has a resemblance to Christian baptism or confirmation.)*

On Thursday I am present at the *kikyoshiki* when the believers get their Buddha name. *Kikyo* means 'to take refuge and respect' and *shiki* means ceremony. It is an occasion where the congregation pledge their Buddhist faith.

In *Amidado* more than 100 names are called up of persons who this day will get their *homyo*. First they are given a big envelope with a kerchief which they take round their shoulders. It takes some time before all the envelopes are handed out. The spectators are friends and relatives, about two hundred of them.

The ceremony begins with a short prayer that all participate in. The *sambo* (Three Treasures): 'I take my refuge in the Buddha, the Dharma and the Sangha' – the Buddhist credo. Then a symbolic tonsure, *o-kamisori*, the removing of hair as a sign that one is a monk. In early Buddhism the shaving of the head accompanied the *sambo*.

Two priests walk up and down the rows. The first has a short prayer for each participant and adjusts the kerchief, after which the other, who is more prominent to judge from his robe, moves a comb-like instrument through the hair, symbolizing a haircut. The latter is one of the Abbot's sons. They work their way through all five rows, walk up to the altar, bow and recite another prayer. Now it is time to give out the *homyo* and each participant gets a new envelope with a small piece of cloth on which the new name is written. The envelopes are opened and read on the spot. Finally, the believers take off their kerchiefs, get up and leave.

It is all very simple and straightforward. To get one's *homyo* at a Ho-onko at the head temple is a serious matter, but there is no air of mystery about it.

In Jodoshinshu a *homyo* consists of two words after either *shaku* (male) or *shakuni* (female) which means 'Buddhist disciple'. The two words are up to the temple to decide and homyo dictionaries are published to help the priests find a fitting *homyo* for the believers. One such example is 'Shaku Chi Shin' in which *chi* means 'wisdom' and *shin* 'faith'.

□

(Saturday is the last day with the most important sermon and superior priests in colourful robes.)

Today the *Goeido* is really crowded. 2-3000 people and organ music over the loudspeakers when I get there. Not funeral music even though it is the day of Shinran's death. Rather there is an atmosphere of expectation. There are no children today, it is simply too crowded. While I wait more and more pilgrims arrive and people sit on the open porch.

The temple bell sounds and it is 9 o'clock. The first sermon begins, based on Shinran's life and the history of Ho-onko. The first Ho-onko was held in 1294 by Kakunyo, Shinran's great-grandson, 33 years after Shinran's death. Kakunyo laid down the rules regarding Ho-onko. The sermon is matter-of-fact and there are not yet any great numbers of priests or musicians. They come during the sermon and also the busy money collectors get ready, even though it is difficult to walk up the rows of the audience.

The preacher – a professor from a Shinshu university in Hokkaido, I am told – rounds off his sermon. The temple priests remove the big sliding door to the porch to make room for all. Today I understand why Higashi Honganji is as big as it is.

The next speaker builds his sermon on the so-called biographical letter by Rennyo from 1477, in which the 'second founder' establishes the position of Ho-onko and gives a brief story of Shinran's life.

Now the money collectors come. About 30 comb the temple although it is difficult to move through the densely-packed crowd.

It is getting close to 10 o'clock when the special *Bando-nembutsu* will be performed. Photographers and cameramen from TVcompanies move into the first rows while the late-comers crane their necks on the porch. Next come the priests and musicians. Also the most prominent priests. A very old man is carried on the shoulders of a young woman – presumably the daughter – to get close.

A single priest in a reddish robe takes up a position in front of the altar and starts burning incense. He is one of the sons of the Otani family. The chorus of priests and musicians begin performing the ancient court music. Just as I think it will be a repetition of last Sunday's antiphonal singing the priests begin moving violently. Sitting, they throw their bodies from side to side, and back and forth. The congregation is delighted. Some laugh and mimic the movements of the venerable priests. Everybody wants to see, many stand up and hinder the view for others. The movements are a repetition of an episode in Shinran's life in which he crossed a lake in an open boat. A gale blew up and the disciples and Shinran rocked the boat through the gale by moving their bodies rythmically. Towards the end of the *bando-nembutsu* amateur photographers get a chance to take pictures as the sequence is repeated.

One-and-a-half hours later – not three hours as announced in the programme – the last ceremony is about to finish. The Otani son leaves first, then the priests and musicians. The pilgrims and other spectators take their leave. The atmosphere is one of joy and delight. Many get their photographs taken on the point of leaving – with the two temples in the background.

Text 31

Ho-onko Time Schedule, November 1992

Source: Office of Ceremonies, Higashi Honganji

SATURDAY, 21 NOVEMBER

1 pm   Meeting on the eve of the anniversary of Shinran's death
          (Taiya Shue)
2   Beginning of the taiya meeting (Taiya hajime)
          Ancient court music (gagaku) (One hour and 40
          minutes) Sutra chanting (Doho hosan) (Shoya (Doho
          hosan)) Sermon (Geike hian)
5   Gates close (Heimon)

SUNDAY, 22 NOVEMBER

5:30 am   Gates open (Kaimon)
6:50   Sutra chanting (Jincho)(50 minutes)
          Sermon on a Rennyo letter (Ofumi howa)
9   Morning meeting (Nicchu shue)
10   Beginning of morning meeting (Nicchu hajime)
          Ancient court music (gagaku)(about 2 hours)
          Ceremony of getting a Buddhist name (Homyo)
          (Kikyoshiki)
          (At Amida Hall)
1 pm   Taiya shue
2   Taiya hajime (One hour)
          Ofumi howa
          Shoya (Doho hosan)
          Geike Hian
5   Heimon

MONDAY, 23 NOVEMBER

5:30 am   Kaimon
6:50   Jincho (Doho showa)
          Ofumi howa

9	Nicchu shue
10	Nicchu hajime (One hour)
	Kikyoshiki (At Amida Hall)
1 pm	Taiya shue
2 pm	Taiya hajime (One hour)
	Ofumi howa
	Shoya (Doho hosan)
	Geike Hian
5	Heimon

TUESDAY, 24 NOVEMBER

5:30 am	Kaimon
6:50	Jincho (Doho showa) (50 minutes)
	Ofumi howa
9	Nicchu shue
10	Nicchu hajime (One hour)
	Kikyoshiki (At Amida Hall)
1 pm	Taiya shue
2	Taiya hajime (gagaku) (One hour and 30 minutes)
	Ofumi howa
	Shoya (Doho hosan)
	Geike Hian
5	Heimon

WEDNESDAY, 25 NOVEMBER

5:30 am	Kaimon
6:50	Jincho (Doho showa) (50 minutes)
	Ofumi howa
9	Nicchu shue
10	Nicchu hajime (gagaku) (One hour and 40 minutes)
	Kikyoshiki (At Amida Hall)
1 pm	Taiya shue
2	Taiya hajime (One hour)
	Ofumi howa
	Shoya (Doho hosan)
5	Shinran's biography (Godensho)(Two hours)
7	Heimon

The Bando Nembutsu, Ho-onko, Higashi Honganji

THURSDAY, 26 NOVEMBER

5:30 am	Kaimon
6:50	Jincho (Doho showa) (50 minutes)
	Ofumi howa
9	Nicchu shue
10	Nicchu hajime (One hour)
	Kikyoshiki (At Amida Hall)
1 pm	Taiya shue
2	Taiya hajime (One hour)
	Ofumi howa
	Shoya (Doho hosan)
	Geike Hian
5	Heimon

FRIDAY, 27 NOVEMBER

5:30 am	Kaimon
6:50	Jincho (Doho showa) (50 minutes)
	Ofumi howa
9	Nicchu shue
10	Nicchu hajime (One hour)
	Kikyoshiki (At Amida Hall)
1 pm	Taiya shue
2	Taiya hajime (gagaku)(One hour and 50 minutes)
	Rennyo's biographical letter (1477) (Gozokusho) (The origin of Ho-onko)
	Shoya (Doho hosan)
	Geike Hian
5	Heimon

SATURDAY, 28 NOVEMBER

5 am	Kaimon
6:30	Jincho (One hour)
9	Nicchu shue
	Sermon in the praise of the virtuous Shinran (Sotoku santan howa)
10	Nicchu hajime (gagaku) (Three hours)
	(The Bando nembutsu)

Text 32

Susu-harai at Higashi Honganji, December 1992

A n advertisement in 'Shinshu', the monthly journal from the main temple, announces that members are invited to participate in *Susu-harai*, 'house-cleaning'. They are encouraged to sign up for the annual cleaning on 20 December.

Susu-harai serves as a good example of a general element in Japanese religions. There is nothing in Shinshu that makes dust an abomination, and fear of what is not clean is normally a Shinto concept. But it is a common phenomenon, as in many New Religions, to purify from dust and dirt. Similarly, in Zen temples floors are washed ritually without being dirty.

On 20 December the volunteers come to the main temple in groups, several hundred, with buses that have started early to be at Higashi Honganji at 8.30 on a Sunday morning. Some have travelled 2-3 hours.

The day begins when a priest welcomes the believers, says a short prayer and the participants sing a psalm. One participant presents a large fan to the priest in charge, and another priest gives information of a practical nature. The groups are called up and split in two: one half for *Amidado*, the other remain in *Goeido*. I notice that the altar is covered with a white cloth, so that the dust will not land on the statues or the altar. Then the participants form a long line as far back in the temple as possible. At intervals in the line there are people who carry huge fans with names that reveal where the followers come from.

Now it all begins. With a loud noise the line of participants beat the *tatami*-mats with bamboo sticks – one in each hand – and the ones with fans fan away the whirling dust. All sliding doors are taken out so there is only one way – out ! The energy is great and a huge cloud of dust rises so that many photographers must wipe the lenses of their cameras afterwards. There is a sense of community, of open and straightforward activity, far from piety.

With pauses every 5-10 minutes the participants beat up the whole temple and reach the porch. In about an hour-and-a-half the cleaning is done.

Susu-harai, *1992, Higashi Honganji*

Kosaiji, Murakami, Niigata, Ho-onko, 1992

Susu-harai takes place close to New Year and is a sign of renewal. On my way home I see many groups of Japanese people outside their houses or blocks of flats engaged in communal cleaning up and removal of leaves and rubbish.

Text 33

Ho-onko at Murakami, Niigata, November 1992

When we get to Murakami it is time for the Ho-onko to start. The kitchen buzzes with at least 10 women who are making preparations. There is a before-the-festival atmosphere, warm and expectant. The name of the temple is *Kosaiji*, 'temple for salvation through light', which refers to Amida Buddha, 'infinite life and infinite light'.

It has been in the possession of the Yasutomi family for four hundred years and its founder was a samurai ancestor who came from the island of Shikoku to the rough climate of Niigata. He was on the losing side in the civil war then, but started a new life as a Shin Buddhist priest.

On the wall in the inner room around the *hibachi*, the open fireplace, there are photographs of the last two priests, the father and grandfather of the 79-year-old priest whose Ho-onko I am visiting. There is also a picture of Shinran who at nine years old left for Mount Hiei, as well as pictures of Kannon, the popular bodhisattva, and the almost inevitable Mount Fuji.

To start with the living: Ryoei Yasutomi, the 79-year-old priest, is a former history teacher and later principal at one of Murakami's high schools. At his father's death, when he himself had retired, he took over. He is still vigorous, has been on pilgrimage to India, Pakistan and Nepal, but next time he wants to go to Paris, which has a special place in the history of the family.

His son is also there, Shinya Yasutomi. In his late forties he is a Professor at Otani University in Kyoto. Being a 'temple boy', as he says, he must break off his academic career when his father is unable to continue. Maybe he would like to continue as a professor, but he owes it to his parents to carry on the temple. In many other instances the hereditary priesthood is of course highly problematic today.

Next the dead, beginning with the grandfather. He was a temple priest exclusively, but very interested in dancing and especially liked to instruct geishas. He was much in demand. He had no son to succeed him, so he adopted a 12-year-old boy from Niigata and arranged the boy's marriage, also at the age of 12.

The adopted son had a long and eventful life. First, he was sent to the most distinguished school in the country, in Tokyo, attended Tokyo University after that, but got pneumonia and became weak. He retired to the temple at Murakami, and when he got better he was summoned to Kyoto by Otani University to become a professor in sociology there. His stay in Kyoto was short and he obained a scholarship at the Sorbonne in Paris. On his return to Japan he became a professor at Yokohama University. Before the age of 60 he retired for the second time to the temple at Murakami. He lived until he was 88.

Although Murakami is off the beaten track, it is not an unenlightened place.

☐

Whether Shinran was at Murakami during his Niigata exile is not clear. The town is old and grew up as a village on the river to the north. Salmon are caught in the river, then and now. But in Shinran's time Niigata was only sparsely populated and was considered miles from anywhere. Sado Island, which is nearby, was used a penal colony. When Murakami grew bigger it merited a castle which was inhabited by a *daimyo*, a local lord. The last daimyo set fire to the castle when the feudal era was over at the beginning of the Meiji period. There have been plans to re-build the castle from the ruins and local politicians want to make it a tourist attraction, but the townspeople protest. After all, it is only 125 years ago that they got rid of the brutal reign of the daimyo.

The temple is not big and the building combines the temple itself and the lodgings of the priest's family. Nearby, there is a bell tower and a small churchyard. Here there are tombs dating back to the Edo period and a typical inscription is 'meeting in one place', that is the Pure Land. Inside the temple there are wooden tablets with names of the families who bury their dead here. When ceremonies are held in the temple, the dead are included in the prayers.

On account of the Ho-onko the illustrations for *Godensho*, Shinran's biography, hang on the inner walls of the temple. Next, you see a picture of Rennyo, the organizer of Shin Buddhism. In the middle a statue of Amida, standing, I am told, because he is active in Shin Buddhism. To the right of Amida there is a picture of Shinran and also a statue of Prince Shotoku, the most significant work of art in the temple. Prince Shotoku has an important function in Shin Buddhism, because he was seen by Shinran in a dream in Kyoto when Shinran left Mount Hiei and spent 100 days in a retreat at Rokkakudo.

□

For the people in the household the Ho-onko begins with a lunch on Saturday. Neither meat nor fish are eaten, and the rice is the new crop. Some consider Ho-onko as a New Year ceremony.

Immediately after lunch the first believers arrive. Those who are absent have sent letters which are registered by the chairman of the congregation. By 2 o'clock about 20 people have turned up, the majority are men, mostly old and no one under 25. Many have *juzu*, rosaries, which they turn between their fingers, and some have bands of cloth around their necks, so-called *wagesa*, symbolic priest's robes. Those who wear *wagesa* are former priests and laymen who have had training in certain religious practices.

The youngest priest comes in first to light the candles, then more and more, and finally there are nine priests, both men and women. They chant *Shoshinge* and some in the congregation join in, supported by small leaflets where the text is printed. In between the hymns you can hear the elder Yasutomi carrying on the ceremony by intoning a new chant. On one occasion the intoning was done by a woman from the congregation. The chanting lasts about an hour.

After a pause, a new priest comes in and having said a brief prayer with the congregation he begins a sermon. His name is Rev. Kusama and in this and two other sermons – Saturday evening and Sunday morning – he deals with man's behaviour when confronted with death, seen in the context of Shinran's death. How to deal with death? Especially how should adherents of Shinran behave? From *Godensho* he tells the audience how Shinran died. According to the biography his death was calm and dignified, but we also have a letter from Shinran's daughter,

Kakushinni, to her mother, Eshinni. Kakushinni was present at Shinran's death, but the wife was not. In Kakushinni's letter she is worried whether Shinran really went to the Pure Land at the moment of death. The mother reassures her in a reply, but the preacher is of the opinion that we might well be in doubt. This leads him to teach the congregation that salvation in Shin Buddhism does not occur at death, but in the middle of life. That is why we should not be concerned whether we die in a dignified way or we die unprepared and in great pain.

In Pure Land Buddhism there has been a strong focus on the moment of death and some who have attended people on their deathbed have debated whether they heard music or saw certain signs, like purple clouds and flowers falling from the heavens, to prove that the person dying really was taken to the Pure Land. One of the old customs was to tie strings between the dying person and an Amida statue or mandala.

□

The preacher's way is kind, he laughs and smiles, and he makes use of the blackboard to explain difficult words or key concepts. Many in the congregation take it down in notebooks. No doubt the preacher is popular, he comes from Niigata city, but has an education from Higashi Honganji and a Shin university in Hokkaido. After three-quarters of an hour he makes a brief pause in which the listeners talk freely. After a stretching exercise to stimulate the circulation of the blood he begins again for another three-quarters of an hour. At about five the programme for the afternoon is over.

After dinner the younger Yasutomi rings the temple bell. He tells me that they do not use the bell as often as before, because people in the neighbourhood complain of the noise.

But the evening belongs to the elder Yasutomi who teaches the congregation about Shinran's life from *Godensho*, which was written in medieval Japanese. This he chants, but in between he translates into modern Japanese in a normal voice register to help the congregation understand.

The preacher takes over again. Sermons are important in Shin Buddhism from the point of view that they are more under-standable than long recitations. It is obvious that the preacher has the attention of most people.

Another way of stimulating believers is to show a video dealing with an episode in Shinran's life as the last item of the day. I am told that the episode is rather unimportant and the presentation a bit overdone, but for people in the congregation who have no education – and certainly did not understand the chanting of *Godensho* earlier – the video as a means of communication is not frowned upon. Around 10.00 o'clock people begin leaving the temple.

□

S unday morning has its first service at 7.30 when 2-3 priests and the elder Yasutomi say morning prayers. Once more *Shoshinge* is chanted. Every day at 7 o'clock there are morning prayers and usually it is the elder Yasutomi alone who says them.

At about 10 o'clock the congregation meet again for the most important ceremony. The house is full of life and the oldest member of the congregation arrives. He gets special treatment and some reassurance when he complains that this is maybe his last Ho-onko. Altogether 10 out of 15 Shin priests in Murakami have met, the candles are lit and I count about 60 people in the congregation.

The service opens with a psalm with organ accompaniment. The organ is played by the elder Yasutomi's wife who when asked says that such music is fairly rare in Shin Buddhism. I assume it may be the result of Christian influence.

Also today letters are registered, both from those absent and from the people present. When opened they turn out to contain money and the amounts are taken down by the chairman with help from the treasurer of the congregation. Like many other Shin Buddhist temples this is privately owned and an important part of the priest's salary is donations like this. Some members give rice as a gift instead.

In the ceremony itself it is the elder Yasutomi who presides. He recites from a scroll. The 90-year-old oldest member of the congregation is sitting on a low chair, the rest on the *tatami*. It is obvious that the oldest member is honoured. During the recitation many members, one by one, go to the incense altar and pray. Otherwise it is the same procedure as yesterday. Mostly the priests sing, and the congregation join in *Shoshinge* and some chant Shinran's *Wasan*, his psalms.

For the last time the preacher takes his turn between 11 and 12 o'clock. The same blend of humour and kind seriousness. One of the other priests places a pocket tape-recorder in front of him. His sermon will give inspiration to the other priests, and the congregation smile and nod approvingly to him. What he says goes.

Suddenly, the whole thing is over. One more psalm accompanied by organ – and now the big banquet.

The congregation have had many meals over the one-and-a-half days but this is the chief meal. First, I am invited to eat together with the priests who are in high spirits and who drink beer and sake. Next, I am sought out by the chairman of the congregation who is very kind and with scraps of English tells me how happy he is. He asserts that to him Shin Buddhism is not only one of many kinds of Buddhism, but is 'true Buddhism'.

I cannot help feeling that I am in very good surroundings.

6 Death and Burial in Shin Buddhism

N ow and then in the international press there are articles about Japanese death and burial customs that surprise the reader. The reasons are connected with ancestor worship which is still very strong in Japan.

The common Japanese belief is that the dead person becomes a *hotoke*, a buddha. In Shinshu, on the other hand, the dead go to the Pure Land and nothing need be done for them. Ancestor ceremonies in Shinshu are, strictly speaking, for the bereaved, whereas in other denominations people believe that they are doing something for the ancestors. For the first 49 days the dead person is in a suspended and dangerous state of existence, and so they are in need of rituals.

Abortions in Japan have a special dimension because certain religions consider the aborted baby's spirit dangerous, so that it must be pacified by religious ceremonies (*mizoku kuyo*). There is a clear element of female oppression in this as it leads to a sense of guilt. For decades access to abortion has been rather easy in Japan.

Shin Buddhism, unlike many other Buddhist denominations, does not share this belief in angry spirits of the dead and so does not encourage *mizuko kuyo* ceremonies.

Dangerous spirits as such, so-called *gaki*, who are spirits of people who have had an unhappy life, and not had proper care in the shape of memorial rites after death, are also thought of as causes of suffering among the living, especially so among the New Religions. That is why they encourage people to hold special ceremonies for them. In this there is a source of income for the sect as all such ceremonies are paid for by the user 100 % – indeed, often more than 100 %!

The latest addition is the *pokkuri dera*, 'temples for sudden death', where old-age pensioners flock. They fear being a liability to their children at a time when families in Japan become more and more nuclear with no room for the elderly. So they wish a healthy old age and some temples assist in this by blessing their underwear at certain special ceremonies or selling them special underwear protecting them against uterine cancer or cancer of the bladder, for instance. Also the elderly wish a sudden death, in order to avoid being a strain for years on their descendants.

According to recent articles *pokkuri dera* can be found in all Buddhist denominations, but mainly in Jodoshu. The Pure Land patriarch, Genshin (942-1017), is said to have founded the *pokkuri* tradition in a chapter in his *Ojoyoshu*, and some of the best known *pokkuri dera* are associated with Genshin.

The concept of *bunkotsu*-tomb, 'a tomb for only parts of the ashes', near the founder's tomb or statue, for instance, is yet another phenomenon, and this is well known in Shin Buddhism – even though, according to tradition, Shinran himself said that he wanted his dead body thrown into the Kamo river as food for fish. In Kyoto there are four central places of ancestor worship in Shinshu Otaniha:

1) Otani Sobyo, at Shinran's tomb in eastern Kyoto, where the new tombs are *bunkotsu*
2) Higashi Otani Bochi, which is the nearby old cemetery with family tombs which today is almost full
3) Shumidan, behind Shinran's statue in Higashi Honganji, see text 36, for *bunkotsu*-tombs only
4) Higashiyama Jo-en, 'The Garden of Purity', established in 1973 by the second son in the Otani family to secure an income to the family independent of Higashi Honganji.

Text 34

Procedure for funerals – excerpts from a handbook for Shinshu priests

Note: There are differences between the various Jodoshin temples.

---

1) Right after the occurrence of death a priest is called and what is popularly known as the 'Pillow Sutra' (*Makura-gyo*), which consists of different parts of gathas, varying from place to place, is chanted. The body is placed so that the head points in the direction north and the face is turned west, the way Shakyamuni died and also Shinran according to the *Godensho*. The dead person's face is covered by a white cloth. The chanting takes place in front of the *butsudan*, not in front of the dead person.

2) A ceremonial washing of the dead body before it is put into the coffin. Today it is performed by an undertaker, but it used to be done by a family member. (*Yukan*)

3) A symbolic shaving of the head takes place to ensure that the dead person becomes a Buddha-person (*hotoke*), and the dead person is given a dharma name (*Homyo*). Ardent Buddhists may have a homyo before, some are also given a homyo as a child. Followed by the chanting of a short *gatha*, the opening verses of *Kuan Wu-Liang-Shou-Ching-Shu* by Shandao. (*Okamisori*)

4) An all-night wake where the close family members and intimate friends are present. It may contain sermons and ceremonies conducted by a priest from the family temple. (*Tsuya*)

5) The coffin is taken to the crematorium, the ceremony of departure. A priest chants sutras, and the family members offer flowers and follow in a procession to the crematorium. (*Shukkan*)

6) At the crematorium the coffin is set down, and the priest burns incense and chants sutras. *Shoshinge* is recited. Also the relatives burn incense. After chanting the dead person is cremated. (*Sojo gongyo*)

7) The next day, or at least after some hours, the ashes are given to the family who with chopsticks pick out bones from the (maybe) still hot ashes and put them into an urn. (*Haiso* or *Shukotsu gongyo*)

8) The return of the ashes and bones in the urn to the dead person's house or temple, and placed in front of the butsudan or altar. Chanting, offering of incense and a simple ceremony during which *Ofumi* (Letters of Rennyo) are read aloud (No 74 in Shinshu Seiten: Chapter on White Ashes) (Ofumi are called *Gobunsho* in Nishi Honganji). (*Kankotsu gongyo*).*

9) After the funeral, memorial ceremonies take place: after 7 days, 14 days, 21 days, 28 days, 1 month (*gakki*), 35 days, 42 days, 49 days, 77 days, 100 days, one year, three years, 7 years, 13 years, 25 years, 33 years, 50 years and 100 years. Mostly these memorial days are held in the temple after which the family members go out for a meal. (*Chuin* for the days, *nenki* for the years).

10) If the dead person's relatives so wish, they can set up a second tomb by opening the first tomb and picking out some bones to be placed in a second small urn and taken to Higashi Otani Mausoleum or Higashi Honganji to be placed close to Shinran's statue.

* If the mourners are many and/or the dead person was well known this ceremony may take place in a temple or it may take place in the home and afterwards in a temple. The names of the mourners may be called out and also telegrams are read aloud.

('*Hikkei – Shinshu Jibutsu no Kaisetsu*' (1978 reprint), by Nishihara Hoshun).
('Handbook – The Explanation on Shinshu Things and Matters')

Text 35

Rennyo: White Ashes – a Letter

R ennyo (1415-99), eighth descendant of Shinran, is the great organizer and champion of Shin Buddhism, often called 'the second founder of Shin Buddhism'. During large parts of his life he was in opposition to the authorities and often actually fleeing from them. He is the builder of many temples and moved the headquarters from place to place. A number of letters from him to the various congregations have survived, the so-called Ofumi which play an important part in ceremonies such as Ho-onko, see texts 30 and 31.

The following text is read at every Shin Buddhist burial and is known by heart by many Shin believers.

あひよしもりてなうふ罪人ほねて
このくのうまこありて古こうくること
苦しぬをうる玉そもとそけにこ
たうか

Details from Scenes from Hell, (TOKYO NATIONAL MUSEUM)

Japanese hearse

Butsudan

Name-plates (ihai)

WhEN we carefully contemplate the transitory aspect of human beings, we usually conclude that, that which is impermanent (like an illusion throughout its beginning, its middle, and its end) is our life-span in this world. Thus, we have never heard of anyone that has had the human body for 10,000 years. One's period of life passes quickly and who today retains the human form for 100 years? Is it I or another that will go first; not knowing whether it is to be today or tomorrow? Life is as fragile as the beads of morning dew clustered around the base of plants and the tiny droplets hanging from the tips of their leaves. We are, therefore, beings that may have faces radiant with life in the morning, and in the evening be white ashes.

No sooner than we are claimed by the wind of impermanency, our eyes are instantly closed. When that one breath can nevermore be had, the radiancy of health alters in vain and we lose the vibrance of life. Our family and relatives then gather and though they may lament in strickened sadness, there can be no altering of the situation. Not able to leave things as they are and after they escort our bodies to the outlying field to vanish as a column of smoke in the middle of the night, only white ashes remain. To say that ours is a most pitiful state hardly begins to describe our true plight.

Therefore, since the transiency of human beings is of this world where both the old and the young alike are impermanent, we should all make haste to place securely within our hearts the prime importance of the life to come in a permanent world and recite the Nembutsu with deep and total reliance upon Amida Buddha.

With reverence, I remain

Text 36

A Shumidan Ceremony at Higashi Honganji, 1993

BEFORE the ceremony the ashes have been divided. The dead person's tomb has been opened and together with the family the local priest has taken some pieces of small bones and ashes. They have been sent to Higashi Honganji with the request that the family get a *bunkotsu*-tomb behind Shinran's statue in Goei-do. *Bunkotsu* means 'part of the bones'. After this the family is told to come on a certain day to participate in the small ceremony when the ashes are installed.

I go to two offices to get permission to witness the ceremony at close quarters. I am taken to a small group of six people, the two families who have paid for the ceremony. They get brief information by a temple priest, and while he is talking two other priests come with two small boxes of untreated wood furnished with the *homyo*, the dead persons' Buddha names. Urns that are only 10 by 10 by 10 centimetres. I follow the two families at a small distance and I am told only to take photos from the back or the side and not behind the Shinran statue. We walk from the office in long corridors to Goei-do and are taken behind the statue. The two boxes are taken over by two other priests and one of them goes into a cupboard-like room behind the statue full of small shelves meant for *bunkotsu*-boxes. While the two boxes are being installed the relatives are told to keep their hands in *gassho*, which is the Buddhist prayer position of the hands. The ceremony is simple and brief.

Next, the small company go out in front of the altar where candles are lit. The priest who has been with the group all the time explains something to them in a low voice. Five priests come, three of them sit down in front of the altar and the remaining two face each other sitting with the statue between them. The latter chant. The relatives do not participate outwardly, but one by one they move to the incense altar and with two fingers they sprinkle powdered incense. Ten minutes later it is over, the five priests leave and the accompanying priest talks to the relatives in a low voice while the candles are extinguished. The participants do not exhibit great emotion, but are serious and are quite likely commemorating the deceased. Probably it is years since he or she died.

The ceremony is over and the two families of three persons each are shown the temple. I myself walk to the office to express appreciation. On my way to the administration building I see the small company in prayer in front of some valuable paintings on a couple of sliding doors.

Text 37

Shin Buddhist Viewpoints on Death and Burial – an Interview

Interview at Otani Sobyo with Rev. Nakatsu Isao on 15 December 1992. Tapescript of questions and answers translated by Prof. Yasutomi Shinya, Otani University.

R ev. Nakatsu: Here at Otani Sobyo we have installed first the ashes of Shinran Shonin, also the ashes of abbots (*monshu*) through history, and the ashes of millions of people who share the beliefs of Jodoshinshu as believers (*monto*). From all over Japan people come to instal ashes and to worship. The ashes are mostly bunkotsu. The numbers of visitors from foreign countries have increased year by year. Those who come have two reasons: to meet the dead member of the family and also to meet Shinran Shonin.

Q: Do ordinary Jodoshinshu followers believe in souls (*tamashii*)?
A: In Shinshu tamashii, meaning souls (*reikon*), is not taught. It is my subjective opinion that there are among ordinary Shinshu believers aspects that have been inherited from their ancestors through the generations, that is the household religion (*ie no shukyo*). These aspects do not necessarily have contact with the teachings of Shinran Shonin. So I can't deny that there are people who believe in the existence of a soul, which is the general belief of the Japanese people. And there are people whose only connection with Shinshu is ancestor worship, but in the tradition of the believers (*monto*) of Shinshu, belief in the tamashii is a spell, an incantation. We have a religious tradition quite free from such superstition. Among the many schools of Buddhism Shinshu is in that sense remarkable.

Q: Would you say that Shinshu is stricter than other forms of Buddhism?
A: Shinshu has since the time of Shinran Shonin been open to the grassroots level, sharing the teaching (*monpo*) with people. It has helped people to live courageously and the result is a big religious movement (*kyodan*). We would have no Shinshu monto in a strict sense in our modern age if we interpreted Shinran's spirit in a narrow way. This realization also makes a new start for each of

us to walk the path of hearing dharma or learning Shinran.

Q: Do you find belief in nirvana (*nehan*) besides belief in the Pure Land among ordinary Shinshu followers?
A: When a closely related person dies, the very natural belief is that the person goes back to the Pure Land. And they will observe us from the Pure Land. Such feelings are intimate with Shinshu people. In daily conversation among Shinshu followers, the word nehan is not used, but essentially nehan and the Pure Land are the same. On the level of daily piety, among farmers and merchants, they don't use concepts such as nehan, but Pure Land.

Q: Do ordinary Shinshu followers believe in a cycle of birth-and-death before they end in the Pure Land – or is there only one life?
A: For myself my life is only once but when my life ends, that is the Pure Land. And so we were taught by Shinran Shonin. The life of delusions finishes with this life. We have no belief in transmigration, in a substantial form of rebirth. But we are told in our sutras that we have been drifting in the ocean of birth-and-death since the beginning of our era (*kalpa*). This term expresses the working of the true dharma which reaches the bottom of delusion at the same time as it expresses the depth of human delusion.

In household Shinshu (*ie no shukyo*) there is maybe a belief in transmigration or rebirth, but only few believe it. We regard it as superstition if we take it as substantial.

Q: What phrase would you use about the rituals concerning ancestors:
    sosen suhai – ancestor worship
    sosen girei – ancestor rites
    sosen saichi – ancestor festivals?
A: *Sosen suhai* we find most natural, but all have the meaning of sosen suhai. In general worship, ancestors are very important, important above all.

Q: It has been discussed whether Japanese ancestor rituals are worship or respect. What is your belief?
A: The problem is how to distinguish between worship and respect. Respect is more human – you may respect people – but when it comes to worship, you are in the realm of a deity, a hotoke or a kami – a transcendental being. It may be a mixture of feeling of both worship and respect when people come here to instal the ashes.

Higashi Otani Bochi

Shinran's mausoleum, Otani Sobyo

Q: According to ordinary Shinshu belief does the dead person become a buddha (*hotoke*) or an ancestral spirit (*sorei*)?

A: Shinshu does not teach that we become hotoke after death. The problem is the salvation of the people who are living now. The problem is how am I to understand the people who have passed away? 'The person who lives true *shinjin*, however, abides in the stage of the truly settled, for he has already been grasped, never to be abandoned. There is no need to wait in anticipation for the moment of death, no need to rely on Amida's coming. At the time shinjin becomes settled, birth too becomes settled.' (Shinran, *Mattosho*, first letter). The stage of the truly settled is also called 'no retrogression into present life' (*gensho-futai*). This means we don't retrogress to the life of delusion again, but 'we are assured of reaching buddhahood' (Shinran). We are emancipated from anxiety about life after death. This means that the life of the nembutsu is open wherever we live and Pure Land is the refuge of human life. Incidentally, Shinran Shonin heard the teaching of Honen and respected him all through his life as the true teacher (*hon-ji*) who manifested himself from within the working of the Wisdom Light, even after he passed away.

Q: The rites of death are similar to the initiation of a monk. Is there a belief that the dead person also becomes a monk in his future life? I am thinking of the symbolic cutting of the dead person's hair (*okamisori*).

A: Okamisori, which is also performed at *Kikyoshiki*, means that the person has left his worldly life and has converted into a new person living under the teachings of Shinshu. It is an expression of that state. Then they are given their Buddhist name (*homyo*) and they are disciples of Sakyamuni while they are living. The homyo given at death is the same. I think its significance lies in the fact that those who did not get a homyo when they lived can get one at death. Through being given this homyo they have the last chance to become the disciple of Buddha and go back to the Pure Land. From the point of view of the family left behind it means that those who have passed away are not extinguished into ashes but return to the world of Buddha and through this they become persons who transmit Buddhas's teachings to those left. I think it has such meaning.

Q: Do you consider the burial and ancestor rituals necessary for the salvation of the dead person?

A: It is both my personal belief and the feeling of people in general that the rituals are very necessary. It is a chance to meet the teachings of Buddha at the point of death. We don't think – and we don't need to say – that those who have died without the funeral rituals are going to hell.

Q: So the rituals are for the dead person's sake?
A: For the people in general they are for the sake of the dead person. These feelings may be strong. A chance for the dead person to meet the teachings of Buddha. But when we go into the rituals and hear the sutras (*dharma*), it is also for the sake of the living, the mourners. It may be a new start in life for some if they can hear the teachings, even though they are in grief. At the same time, in this way the dialogue with the dead person becomes deepened limitlessly.

Q: Visits to graves (*haka mairi*) according to a recent book are increasing in Japan. Is that also the case in Shinshu?
A: Yes. We have very many visitors especially at O-bon and at O-higan. They may come to perform *sosen suhai*. But in Shinshu we have *Ho-onko* for meeting the teachings of Shinran Shonin. To those who are Shinshu monto, *Ho-onko* is the most important Buddhist event.

Q: Are ceremonies for abortions (*mizuko kuyo*) performed at Otani Sobyo or other Shinshu temples?
A: We don't. There are people who come for the purpose of *mizuko kuyo* at O-bon and O-higan. We tell them that we in Shinshu don't have *mizuko kuyo*, but they don't accept the answer. We sometimes advise them to accept sutra recitation. If they agree to this, we accept them, but that does not mean that we agree with their wish for *mizuko kuyo*. Then, in case they accept sutra recitation, we write the *homyo* (or the name of the dead child) on a *homyo ita*, which is a piece of wood. Because we wish that those who come for a *mizuko kuyo* and accept the sutra recitation may have a chance to hear the teachings of nembutsu, this is what we do.

Q: Are ceremonies for 'hungry spirits' (*segaki-e*) performed in Shinshu?
A: No, we don't have segaki-e in Shinshu. Those who want *segaki-e* are very few.

Q: Do you get requests from families who wish to change the position of a grave because they have been told so by, for instance, a new religion? If yes, do you comply with their requests?

A: Almost nobody wants to change the position of the graves here. For those who want a new tomb, we have in reality no new sites left at Higashi Otani cemetery (*bochi*), but some tombs have been returned or some are unknown, and when we put them in order, we may find place for a new tomb. Generally speaking, almost all Japanese people build tombs, but we don't mention anything about the position or shape of the tombs. We in Shinshu are not bound by superstition.

Q: Are the dead whose ashes are at Otani Sobyo all Jodoshinshu followers and is it a requirement?

A: In the case of this *sobyo*, everybody is welcome. In the case of the Higashi Otani cemetery (*bochi*) the individual tombs are limited to members only.

Q: Do you offer written advice to the families on how to tend the graves?

A: Otani Sobyo has no special written advice, except a brochure, 'Otani Sobyo', which I will give you. It differs in shape only from the one from Higashi Honganji. Besides, we inform and recommend the monto to read a guidebook 'A Guide to Serve Family Altars', published by Higashi Honganji, about how to perform various Shinshu rites and participate in events.

Rev. Nakatsu Isao: I want to conclude by adding that those who come here offer fruit, flowers, sake, beer and other things. We realize that it is a place for our visitors where they feel close to their dear departed – a dead wife, a dead husband, dead children – but for us, apart from these very human feelings, we cannot but hope that we can offer a chance and occasion for them to hear the teachings of Shinran Shonin and to live under the teachings of nembutsu, above all.

7 Shin Buddhist Education

When the Meiji government in 1868 opened the country to the West and abolished the privileged position of Buddhism, the Buddhist religions found out that they needed to know more about the development of Buddhism in order to match modern Western history of religions. Until then the Japanese had concentrated on Chinese sources and the Chinese did not develop Indian studies once the texts were translated. Moreover, the 250 years of isolation during the Tokugawa period were not conducive to foreign languages studies.

To solve that problem the Buddhist sects sent students to Europe, for instance the Otani denomination sent two students to France and England, especially to Oxford to study under Max Müller, then the leading scholar in Sanskrit, the ancient holy language of India. Nanjo Bunyo (1848-1927) was one of those students. (The other was Kasahara Kenju – 1852-83 – who died young). It was Nanjo Bunyo who introduced modern Sanskrit studies to Japan and taught at Otani University, where he became the second president. He is the compiler of the so-called 'Nanjo Catalogue', a register of Chinese Buddhist texts.

Also, Tibetan studies have a long tradition at Otani University. In 1900 Enga Teramoto discovered a bulky volume of the Tibetan Tripitaka in Beijin, and offered the manuscripts to Otani University. Aften studying in Tibet, he was invited to become a professor at Otani in 1915 and gave his first lectures on Tibetan studies there. Much later, the university published a photographic reproduction of the Beijin edition of the Tibetan Tripitaka in 168 volumes in the 1950s. And recently a former Tibetan monk was employed as professor at the university.

However, to suggest that Shin Buddhist education did not start until the Meiji era is not altogether true, as the universities did not start out as universities but evolved from institutions to train the Buddhist clergy during the Tokugawa period.

As is the case of other sects in Japan, Shinshu Otaniha runs a number of schools and colleges. Of these, besides Otani University, Otani High and Junior High School and the Senshu Gakuin have been singled out for presentation. The latter is the alternative theological seminary to Otani University. At Nishi Honganji, the counterpart institutes of higher learning are Ryukoku University, with a history of 350 years, and Kyoto Women's College. In addition, they also run a number of primary and secondary schools throughout Japan.

Text 38

Kiyozawa Manshi: *Opening Ceremony Address of Shinshu University (1901)*

*A*t Otani University there is a long tradition for two lines of ideas: Kiyozawa Manshi's ideas of a university based on faith, spirituality and independence, and those of Nanjo Bunyo (and Sasaki Gessho, the third president) of culture and objective learning with no sectarian strings. At the time Otani University opened as Shinshu College in 1901 the aim was to educate for the nation, otherwise it would not be recognized as a university at that time. Before then it served the temples mainly and gave edification, not education. As a matter of fact it started as a seminary for priests in 1665.

Still, at the time of the beginning of the modern period in 1901, it had two aims: to educate both for the temples and for the nation.

To aim at the temples only would be against the principles of education of the time. In 1901 the Imperial Rescript on Education had existed for 10 years. It was read at the opening of Shinshu University, significantly not by Kiyozawa Manshi but by Nanjo Bunyo. Kiyozawa came close to committing an outrage in 1893 when he wrote an article about the aims of university education in which he advocated neither personal benefit nor divine order (the Emperor), but faith.

Today we enjoy the great privilege and honour of celebrating the event of moving into the new premises of Shinshu University, in the presence of distinguished guests from the government as well as from society at large. It is not, however, the beginning of the University, but it has been moved from the old location in Kyoto to a new building here.

The main principles of the University can be studied elsewhere, but this University differs from other universities in being a School of Religious Studies, especially devoted to Jodoshinshu Buddhism. Based upon *hongantariki* (primal vow and other power) and our deeply cherished *nembutsu*-faith, this University is especially designed to foster personalities who devote themselves to transmit this faith to others, to the awakening of faith, which is our greatest event in life.

The University consists of a two-year introduction period followed by three years of the main study. Thus a student graduates after five years. Afterwards, especially qualified students may be selected for postgraduate courses ranging from three to five years.

As to contents, specialized teaching in one religious tradition will be offered, as well as the teaching of a variety of religious doctrines and other related subjects considered important to society.

Not daring to claim perfection, but relying upon the powers inherent in our priests and the lay-people, and supported by friends from outside, we will, in the spirit of the Buddhist Founder (Shinran Shonin), strive to attain our goals.

Text 39

Shin Buddhist Viewpoints on Education – an Interview

Interview with President Terakawa Shunsho, Otani University, which took place on 13 February 1993. Tapescript of questions and answers translated by Prof. Yasutomi Shinya, Otani University.

Q: To begin with it may be a good idea to know your opinion

about the general state of affairs regarding education in Japan.

A: There are some problems in Japanese education in present-day Japan. When new students come from high schools I have some contact with them. Our university, as you know, has a religious tradition and so we are interested in that aspect in our students. We as a Buddhist university are interested in the spiritual exploration of man, not the exploration of God. 'What is man? Who am I?' But these questions do not interest the students I meet. Their concern is to get an education, to score high marks. They have almost no interest in religion. They have not had a chance to think about the meaning of life. They have a 'how-to' concern and want to enjoy life. Later to get a good profession. Their interests are very secular. This is the result of the public education in Japan. From the beginning of the Meiji period, almost 120 years ago, in order to build a modern nation, the public school system has found no time to educate in religion. Religious education is forbidden. So we have got a secularized nation. This is a very great problem for a religious university. About a quarter of private universities are religious and among them the most numerous are Christian (Sophia University and Doshisha University, for instance).

As you know, Japanese Buddhism is divided into many streams. The main streams are Nichiren, Zen, Shingon (with many esoteric, primitive, but very popular practices), and Jodo and Jodoshinshu. Of these Pure Land Buddhism has been called 'the essence of Buddhism' by D.T. Suzuki and is to me the true and pure form of Buddhism. All through the history of Japan until modern times, Shinran's Buddhism has transmitted the right form of Buddhism. That is our conviction. Shinran was very critical of especially magical, esoteric Buddhism.

I think it is permissible to see Shin Buddhism as the form of Buddhism that has best preserved the essence of Buddhism.

Q: From the English brochure presentation of the university, and from talks, I know about the two basic ideas behind Otani University: Kiyozawa Manshi and his emphasis on 'the Shin Buddhist faith' and 'personal involvement', and Sasaki Gessho's educational aims of 'the objective study of Buddhism, free from narrow sectarian viewpoints'. Is there any reason to revise these aims today and strike a new balance?

A: Kiyozawa Manshi was a truth-seeker and the founder of the university and Sasaki Gessho was an excellent mahayana scholar.

They may seem different but are both in the tradition. Kiyozawa Manshi thought about his own salvation, and Sasaki Gessho thought most about studying and teaching Buddhism. They grew up under different conditions. But both were educators and to both education meant human education, that is education which forms the human being. The same with Shinran Shonin who brought Buddhism to the people. Kiyozawa lived at a time when Shinran's soteriology had to be redefined under very difficult conditions. Sasaki was a student of Kiyozawa and followed suit in Kiyozawa's interests, but his situation was different. Kiyozawa is Meiji (1868-1912), Sasaki is Taisho (1912-1926).

Q: What is your own attitude? Where do you stand yourself?
A: Shinran lived in the thirteenth century but his teachings did not become popular until Rennyo in the fifteenth century. Then about 80 years later Francis Xavier and Christianity came to Japan.

Rennyo was very influential in the transmission of Shinran's teachings. After Rennyo it was the time of the *ikko ikki* (peasant revolts), and in this time of war Shogun Oda Nobunaga (1534-82) suppressed religion and defeated the peasant revolts. The strong spirits of Shinran and Rennyo became very weak in the Tokugawa period in Jodoshinshu. The religion turned very pious, quiet and obedient to the authorities. It was the period of Japan closing its doors to the rest of the world. In the original form of Shinshu, we are born into the Pure Land. But in the Edo period, the Pure Land was relegated to another world, to after death. And Amida was thought of as a transcendental saviour.

Then with the Meiji period, Kiyozawa appeared and knew about the philosophies of Hegel and other Europeans through his professor at Tokyo University, Ernest Fenellosa. His studies were not limited to Japan and in this he was a very representative Meiji intellectual. To him the old Shinshu tradition was very difficult to believe in. Kiyozawa had to rediscover Shinran to find out how modern people are saved.

I feel more intimately connected with Kiyozawa than with Sasaki Gessho. Professor Sasaki was an educator and the president when the Universities Act was passed in 1922, and he fitted Otani University into the requirements of a university then. He took his model from Oxford University. He respected Nanjo Bunyo and the textual studies of sanskrit, pali and Tibetan, and, of course, Chinese. He stood for modern buddhology and this university started such studies. He introduced modern methods to make the rather narrow Japanese Buddhist studies broader. But at the same time he was an educator wanting to educate young people to know themselves.

I, as a president of this university, very much admire Sasaki Gessho's work, but as a private person I feel the debt to Kiyozawa Manshi stronger. Also my own teacher was Soga Ryojin who was a disciple of Kiyozawa.

Q: In your period as president you have initiated two new developments so far: Next year you will start 'International Studies' at Otani. And last year Otani started obligatory courses in *ningengaku* (anthropology) based on Buddhism. What are the ideas behind?

A: About ningengaku we follow the frames set out by the ministry of education (Mombusho). We put great emphasis on education, rather than research. We want to offer opportunities to all students to learn to understand themselves. What is a human being and what is life? Ningengaku's aim is to give the students such opportunities. It is very important. As I said before, the students have almost no education in such questions.

Buddhism is very much the exploration of the human being. So instead of calling it Buddhist studies, it is more relevant to call it ningengaku.

International studies are based on the curriculum from Japanese national universities in their faculties of humanity. They consist mainly of philosophy, history and literature. We have a Buddhist university so we add studies of Shinran and Shin Buddhism as a basic component. In literature we have departments in English and German, besides Japanese and Chinese. In the present day of internationalization, we must think international. What we must add are general cultural components, international culture. We have a good background already in oriental studies: China, Tibet, India. Buddhism is not only worship, but also a very rich culture. Buddhism itself is international. And when we study Buddhism internationally, at the same time we learn what Japanese Buddhism is, seen in perspective.

The combination of our studies (majors) offered and the courses in ningengaku means that although we specialize in many subjects, we are all human beings. On the one hand we are researchers, on the other hand we are human beings. Shakyamuni rejected the caste system because we are all human beings. But more details about the international studies I cannot give you, because we have not yet started.

Q: Is the ningengaku in the spirit of Kiyozawa Manshi and the International Studies in the spirit of Sasaki Gessho? Can you say that?

A: Kiyozawa was a very representative Meiji figure. He was among the first to study European philosophy. In that he also met the question raised by the Greeks, 'Know yourself'. Kiyozawa's eyes were open to the world. He also wanted his students to be international although in a very small university. When Kiyozawa studied at Tokyo University the lectures were in English and French.

Q: A university which is both a school for becoming Shinshu priests and for students seeking a variety of occupations may attract a particular type of student. How many come from Shinshu background to seek an education as a priest, and how many come with a variety of motives?

A: As far as I know about 16-20 % of the graduates go into priesthood or missionary activities. As for the families and their religions, it is very difficult to answer. They mostly come from the Kinki area (West central Honshu) where there are many Shinshu members. But we have no figures. According to a recent investigation, however, on the degree of satisfaction with universities, on questions like characteristics of the university and aim of education, Otani University has a very good position. Out of 200 universities Otani takes up positions between 10 and 16 in the various questions. We can see that our image as a Buddhist university is rather strong among our students. Many come because they know us as a Buddhist university.

Q: How many faculty members are ordained Shinshu priests and is it a requirement for some posts?

A: About 20 %. As for the position of President, priesthood ordination is customary, but it is not a requirement according to our constitution. There are some religious ceremonies that a president has to lead, and so it is convenient that the president is ordained.

Q: What is the connection between Otani University and lower ranging schools in the Shinshu Otaniha denomination?

A: The Otaniha denomination has this university, Kyushu Otani University, Otani High School and Junior High School in Kyoto and others. They are all established by the Otaniha denomination.

With Otani High School we have a special connection. About 40 students come from that school every year. In total, there are 18 Shinshu high schools in the country. Also there are some training schools for ministers. All share the same religious attitude and we provide training for those responsible for religious education in the other schools. We have exchange of information and conferences between headmasters, but the coordination role belongs to the *honzan* or head temple. Our cooperation is not so tight, however.

Q: One final question: In the beginning you deplored the fact that the high school graduates come here with no religious education. How can this be changed?

A: The role we can play is to use religious ceremonies, commencement and graduation ceremonies, for instance. In such ceremonies I talk directly to the students. We also invite guest speakers from outside to give lectures for all students, lectures with religious content. Lately, we have invited a sociologist and a novelist. Then we have *ningengaku*, as we have talked about. We want to offer as many opportunities as possible. But it is not so easy.

We hope that after they graduate, they will keep Shinran, Tannisho and Shinshu in mind – in whatever profession they have. We know that Otani University graduates have a good reputation for being sincere people.

Text 40

The Theological Seminary: Senshu Gakuin, Yamashina

A summary of an interview with Rev. Nakagawa on 16 February 1993. Prof. Yasutomi Shinya, Otani University, acted as an interpreter.

Rev. Nakagawa: By far most students come to get the education and then apply for a certificate to become Otaniha priests from Higashi Honganji. That takes one year. But they can stay another year if they wish.

The subjects they are taught are first and foremost *shinshu-gaku* (Shinshu studies) and Shinran, but also other courses are obligatory, such as Philosophy and the Study of Religions. (The latter means Christianity and the subject is taught by an Italian Catholic who graduated from Otani.) Other courses are optional, for instance Music, Calligraphy and *ikebana* (flower arrangement). The Senshu used to have more subjects, for instance Sociology, but decided to cut down because it was too much for the students.

The students come almost all from temple families or because they will marry into temple families. They come from Hokkaido to Kyushu as there is only one school of its kind. Their educational backgrounds differ widely, but many come right after high school. Some are married, most are not, and the ages are between 18 and 70 with an average of 25. Ten are females out of the 84 enrolled and three other females follow courses in their second year. The school has a limit of 100 students and this year it has 84 students. The yearly average is 60, but there has been a growth in the last few years.

The students are thought to be well-motivated, also compared to Otani students, but of course the one-year study for priesthood has less prestige than Otani University. There are exams at the end, but all pass.

The students and the teachers, all ages and both sexes, live in a dormitory about 10 minutes from the school. The educational philosophy is that of 'learning together' in a *dojo*-community (dojo – Buddhist training hall) in a *dobo*-spirit (spirit of religious comradeship). The educational philosophy was founded by a respected educator, not only in Shinshu education, but in Japan as such, called Nobukuni Atsushi who died 14 years ago. He planned the curriculum and re-organized the school in 1958 along the lines of 'hearing and responding', i.e. hearing Buddha's teaching and responding thereto. Since the re-organization about 2000 students have graduated from the Gakuin of whom over 1800 are alive and receive the newsletters from the school. (2000 out of more than 16,000 Otaniha priests means 10-15%, but some are educated at both Otani University and Senshu Gakuin.)

The community life is rather strict and zen-like. All get up at 6.30am, clean the dormitory, go to school where they have morning service, then breakfast and classes until 3.00pm, from 3.00 to 5.00 they are free, and then at 5.00 another service and evening meal. Students and teachers share the cooking jobs. Twice a week they have evening meetings based on *Tannisho*, usually lead by the President of the school and followed by discussions.

Text 41

Religious Education at Otani High and Junior High School

A summary of an interview with Rev. Ikeda Masataka, head of Religious Education on 17 March 1993. Prof. Yasutomi Shinya, Otani University, acted as an interpreter.

Rev. Ikeda Masataka: At Otani High and Junior High Schools there are 1700 students, and 80 teachers of whom eight are Shinshu priests. Kiyozawa Manshi was the first headmaster of the school and it was his first experience as a head of school.

In both High and Junior High Religious Education has one hour (50 min) per week, which is obligatory. It is a substitute for *dotoku* (ethics) but it also contains some elements of *dotoku* in that it teaches some ethical matters.

In Otani High School all three years have textbooks in Religion, but not so in Otani Junior High where the teacher hands out material. The textbooks are not approved by the Ministry of Education (*Mombusho*), but are decided upon by the teachers in Religious Education. They are published by the Otaniha School Association. The first is called *Tomoshibi* (meaning 'torch') and is meant as a general introduction to human life, to questions of how to live. It is taught in a two-teacher system and the slow learners are given a second book which focuses on life in a community.

The second year has a book on Indian Buddhism, produced by the school itself. The third year uses a book called *Shinran no michi* ('Shinran's way'), also an Otaniha School Association book. It deals almost exclusively with Shinran's life.

Besides the obligatory one hour per week there is also a religious hour once a week where students gather in the lecture hall according to their year in school and are given lectures by teachers on a broad variety of subjects. In that sense they have two hours per week.

Moreover, there are optional classes, also during normal school hours. Students must choose between various alternatives, among them is an enlarged course on religions.

Students are very much interested in intellectual development – and in sports. They don't take much interest in religion in a narrow sense, but like to know about life and thinking, about life questions in general.

About the treatment of religion in textbooks approved by the Ministry of Education (*Mombusho*)? There is no special Mombusho attitude towards religion. Mombusho is indifferent, and nowadays Mombusho wants each school to profile itself. Today, more than in the past, Religious Education has been given more freedom. It started four years ago when the schools were allowed to give Religious Education in the second year also. As it is now, the hours correspond with the interests of the students. And they are satisfied, as far as can be seen. When students graduate they tell the younger ones that they are satisfied with Religious Education.

As to the prestige of Religious Education teachers: In a private religious school they are treated the same way as other teachers, there is no difference. How it is in public schools, is maybe another matter.

Shinran Shonin. Modern woodblock print from a school-book at Otani High School

8 Shin Buddhist Mission in Hawai'i

The Japanese in Hawai'i have a dramatic history. The first group of immigrants from Japan came in 1868 to work in the sugar plantations, but it was not until 1885 that government supervised immigration started and grew to surprising dimensions. The first Shinshu priest (from Nishi Honganji) came in 1889 to establish Shin Buddhism in the Christian-oriented islands. Towards the turn of the century, when the Japanese constituted 40 % of the total population, more missionaries came, also one from Higashi Honganji, but Nishi Honganji is by far the main thrust of Shin Buddhism. Among the early leaders Bishop Yemyo Imamura deserves special mentioning. He became a spokesman for Buddhism from 1899 until his death in 1932, and was held in high regard because of his activities in settling labour disputes, establishing Japanese language schools and, in general, explaining Buddhism to the larger Hawaiian community. Some Christians, however, saw the language schools as a threat to the American way of life, and held that Buddhism and Americanism were contradictory.

Hawai'i became an American territory in 1900 and from about 1907-8 no more single male Japanese were allowed to immigrate. Between 1908 and 1924 only parents, wives and children of the immigrant males were allowed to settle. In 1940 the Japanese population of *issei* (first generation), *nisei* (second generation) and *sansei* (third generation) accounted for 37 % of Hawai'i's population.

Although the Japanese were many, they found themselves as a minority group experiencing various forms of discrimination and pressures. To them it was necessary to hold on to the customs, faith and loyalties which they brought with them. Buddhist temples became social centres and the teaching a source of consolation for those undergoing the hard life of the plantations and later factories.

Buddhist temples also attempted to adapt their services to meet the needs of the new environment, manifesting the flexibility that had characterized the spread of Buddhism across Asia. They early on employed organs, pews, hymns, sermons, Sunday school classes and weddings. Much of the adaptation was pioneered by Bishop Imamura, who believed that Buddhism was a universal faith and should be accessible to those outside Japanese culture.

Still, Buddhism in the American scene was in a defensive posture. It was confused with Shinto by Christians who also resented them for being resistant to conversion. As World War II was drawing near the Americans in Hawai'i were suspicious of the loyalty of the Japanese.

Then catastrophe occurred: the attack on Pearl Harbour on 7 December 1941. The whole population group became hostages and their leaders were sent to mainland America for internment together with 112,000 Japanese, mainly from the US West Coast.

After the War the Japanese in Hawai'i became more integrated and some gained influential positions in politics and society. At the same time more problems arose for the established Buddhist missions, although some Japanese rituals live on.

One of the main problems is that a sect like Shinshu Otaniha is too small in numbers to raise its own priests, so the members of the sect have to make do with missionaries sent from headquarters in Japan. These missionaries often have big language problems. Also the wages are small for Buddhist priests compared to Catholic priests, for instance. It should be added, though, that Honpa Honganji has some thirty temples and as many priests, besides a Buddhist Study Center on the University of Hawai'i campus.

Around 1930 Honpa Honganji (Nishi Honganji), which is by far the biggest Japanese religion in Hawai'i, had about 100,000 members, but today only 21,500. Shinshu Otaniha (Higashi Honganji) today has about 1800 in a society which is a supermarket in religions: 21 Buddhists sects, 28 Protestant sects (besides Roman Catholic and other Christian sects) and many New Religions.

(Source: Department of Religion, University of Hawai'i, 1982.)

Text 42

Hazama Tatsuyo: *Young Picture Bride*

*B*etween 1908 and 1924 the single men in Hawai'i, who wanted to marry a woman from Japan, were allowed to do so, but the woman could not go to Hawai'i before the marriage. This led to the custom of 'picture marriage' (sashin kekkon).

In 1919, when I was an eighteen-year-old living in the Hiroshima countryside, a *nakahodo* came to ask my parents for my hand in marriage to a young man in far away Hawai'i. The *nakahodo* brought a picture of a young man standing in a dark American suit. I'll never forget walking very far with my mother to have my picture taken to send to Hawai'i. When we and our families had agreed on the marriage, it was recorded in the *Koseki Tōhon* in Hiroshima. I had no problem in accepting the arrangement because it was the Japanese custom for parents and the *nakahodo* to arrange the marriages.

After a simple *shashin kekkon*, picture marriage, I went to live with my in-laws for six months. This, too, was the custom, but I was so unhappy because I had to work very hard in my in-laws' home. I was like a servant; no, my life was worse than a servant's. So I ran away to my family several times, but each time, my in-laws and the *nakahodo* came to plead with me to return to their household. Since I was the *chōnan's* (oldest son's) bride, they said I had to stay with them for six months. Some dejected picture brides refused to return to their in-laws' houses and were registered as divorced before they ever met their husbands.

After six months, my father-in-law accompanied me and a young sixteen-year-old picture bride for my husband's brother, to the port city of Yokohama. We travelled by *jinricksha*, a small carriage pulled by a man, and by train to the port city. It was my first train ride and my first view of the ocean! I was excited about the trip so I didn't worry about what my new husband would be like. The young girls in my village wanted to have the opportunity to travel.

The *funachin*, boat fare, was $53.00, and we had to pass an inspection to show that we were free of diseases. Once on board the *Shunyo Maru*, the brides showed off the photographs of their husbands. I was so ignorant about the trip that I had packed my clothes and my husband's picture in the trunk which was taken from me and stored in the hold. I was so embarrassed because the other brides teased me and wouldn't believe that I had packed his picture away.

Most of the trip on the *Shunyo Maru* was miserable. I was so seasick that I couldn't eat. The trip to Honolulu took eight days. I was too sick to get up so I lay on my bunk for six of those days. Just as I began to feel better, our ship reached Honolulu Harbor. By then I was suffering from the heat because I had to wear the heavy kimono which I had on when I boarded since my things were in storage.

As we docked, I looked down and recognized my husband from the photograph; but we were not allowed to meet or talk together for about a week. We were taken straight to the immigration station for another inspection. We were all afraid of the inspector who was Japanese for he talked loudly, scolded everyone, and ordered us around. Once, he grabbed my hairdo and said: 'Get rid of your *nezumi* (rat).' It was the style to wear a high hairdo with a cushion inside to give it body, so I had one of these in my hair.

When the day finally came for us to meet our husbands, we excitedly helped to dress each other in a *montsuki*, special kimono with a crest, and a fancy sash called a *maruobi*. Outside the immigration station, our husbands waited eagerly for a glimpse of us. We were nervous and shy. I thought my husband was tall and handsome. We rode in a two-horse carriage to Onomichiya Hotel. The next day, my husband and his brother took us to see Waikīkī.

Two days later, we went by boat to Līhue, Kaua'i, to live on the plantation. We were already married in Japan, but we did have a party. The people in the camp prepared the food for the celebration which was held in the social hall.

One month after arriving in Hawai'i, I was expected to go out to the fields to work. A friend made me a shirt, skirt, and apron, and arm protectors; and I did *hoe hana*. Later, I had the job of putting foot-long pieces of sugar cane into bags for planting. If the bags were not full enough, we were scolded and told to fill the bags again. Some luna were strict and shook the bags hard to make the stalks settle way down. Others were kind and gave the ladies a wink and went on. I was young so I was a pretty good worker. When I became pregnant, I went to Honolulu to learn a skill. I boarded there for six months while I learned to sew so that I wouldn't have to labour in the hot sun with my children.

Tatsuyo Hazama, Age 83
Interviewed in 1978 and 1984

(*Okage Sama De – The Japanese in Hawaii*
ed. by D.O. Hazama & J.O. Komeiji,
(Bess Press, Honolulu, 1986))

Text 43

Kikuchi Shigeo: *7 December 1941*

The historic date, 7 December 1941, needs few comments. To the Japanese in Hawai'i it meant that they were made collective hostages.

The night before 7 December 1941, we honoured the elders of the temple at a Bodhi Day celebration sponsored by the YBA members. Early the next morning, I sent my husband off to Hilo to attend the opening meeting of the education committee at Hilo Betsuin. While I was preparing for my Sunday school service, Mr Hamada, the YBA president, dashed in and said, 'Okusan, an awful thing has happened. There is a rumour that Japan has bombed Pearl Harbor.' I was shocked and disbelievingly turned on the radio. Unmistakably an announcer was confirming that this terrible thing had occurred. The announcer went on to give details of the great confusion in Honolulu. As the innocent children came for Sunday school, I told them, 'We will not have Sunday school service today; and you must go home.' Shocked and fearful at hearing of the Pearl Harbor attack, many people came to the temple seeking advice.

My husband came home from Hilo in the afternoon. He said that they, too, were not aware of the incident at the morning meeting but just as they were about to have lunch, a message was received stating that war had broken out between Japan and America and that everyone should return home immediately. This was shocking information. Panic-stricken, the ministers left Hilo with empty stomachs.

We were warned that lights were to be made invisible from our houses but every household was not prepared to handle this situation. Even when a tiny streak of light was seen, the soldiers from a guardpost came and issued warnings.

At midnight, someone knocked at the door. My husband got up to answer the knock and found a Hawaiian police officer friend standing at the door. 'Rev. Kikuchi, I want you to come to the office for a minute.' My husband left with him but soon after returned home. The policeman told him, 'I want you to go to Volcano and because it is cold there you should take some warm clothing and put them into a bag. After changing his clothes, he picked up the 'Shinshu Seiten' from the bookcase and put it in his pocket. As he left he said, 'There is nothing to worry about, I will return in two or three days. But I want you to inform the resident Japanese that we are now in an unexpected situation. Because we are governed by the United States everyone must respect and obey the law of the government and continue to work earnestly. Whatever happens, be patient, control yourself, and never argue or fight with people of other ethnic groups. As for me, nothing to worry about because I have done nothing wrong. After this investigation is over, I will come home.' Then he disappeared into the darkness with the officer.

Early the following morning, Mr Beatty, the plantation boss, came and comforted me, saying, 'Mrs Kikuchi, the situation between the United States and Japan has become bad, but I think that Reverend Kikuchi will be coming home soon.' After saying this, however, he requested that all of the Japanese-American men, regardless of whether they were first or second generation, report to the Japanese language school at 2 o'clock that afternoon. I immediately telephoned those persons in charge of Waiohinu, Honuapo, and Hiilea, using the plantation boss's home phone.

The war had changed our friendly climate overnight. We were now considered enemies. It caused me great pain to face members from other ethnic groups. So with a heavy heart, I went again to the home of the plantation boss. His wife said, 'Mrs Kikuchi, war is between the United States and Japan; not you and me.' Her compassionate words struck me and tears began to flow from my eyes. I humbly asked her to convey my message to the persons in charge of the Miss Taylor Camp, Puumakani, Waiubata, Kaalaiiki, and Ninole by telephone. This was done and that afternoon at 2 o'clock, all first and second generation Japanese-American boys gathered at the designated Japanese Language School building.

Mr Beatty, the plantation boss said, 'Gentlemen of Japanese

ancestry, it is regrettable that war exists between the US and Japan. Because we are living in America we must respect American law. I would like you to continue to work earnestly and peacefully. Never argue or fight with members of other ethnic groups.'

'Both Reverend Kikuchi and Mr Suzuki have been taken to Volcano Army camp,' he continued, 'but I think they will be coming home soon.' After Mr Beatty spoke, I humbly asked for an opportunity to convey my husband's message to the Japanese people of Naalehu. If this had been an ordinary day, several members would have remained after the meeting to socialize in our living room but today, everyone went home. I was there alone; thinking about what I should do, when I realized it was way past sunset, and the sky was dark.

As soon as the investigation was over, I had hoped that my husband would be home, but I waited a week, then two weeks, and yet he did not return. Perhaps by Christmas, I thought. Maybe by New Year's. My hopes and expectations were in vain. I received no word from him.

As an enemy alien, my bank savings account and my checking accounts were frozen, and I suffered a great deal.

The most difficult situation for me at the time was being unable to send funds for tuition to my son Akira who was studying on the mainland. One day I received a letter from Akira which read, 'I deeply regret that war has broken out between Japan and the United States. Father and Mother, you must be at an awful loss, but please try not to worry about me. I am always with the Buddha. Even if you are unable to send me money, I will work as a schoolboy and go to school.' While I was relieved and happy at reading this letter, I was concerned about him. I knew he needed money to buy his winter clothing. While worrying about Akira, a second letter arrived. It read, 'Mother, you have always written to your friends to ask them to look after me but now I am the one who is in a position to look after them, so please do not send such a letter.'

During the war, Japanese-Americans on the mainland were evicted from their homes with only a single suitcase. This I learned later on. I also learned that Akira became a school boy right after the outbreak of war. When Akira learned that his father was transferred to the mainland, he brought his father his favourite past-time game, 'go' which consisted of a board and stones, 'go-ban' and 'go-ishi'. During my husband's four years of internment, this game helped console him and his friends.

Later on we learned that in April of 1942 students such as Akira who were studying on the mainland were also assembled in camps. When grammar and high schools were started for the children interned there, Akira was employed as a teacher in the high school for which he received a small salary. Before long, interned individuals were allowed to volunteer for the Army. Akira volunteered but was not accepted because of a previous appendicitis operation. However, through a friend's intercession, he became an instructor of Japanese language at a military school for the duration of the war.

(*Memoirs of a Buddhist Woman Missionary in Hawaii*,
by Kikuchi Shigeo (Buddhist Study Center Press,
Honolulu, 1991). pp. 34-38).

Text 44

Mr David Kobata: *Memoirs of a Japanese Buddhist in Hawai'i – an Interview, 5 February 1993*

Q: Could you give a brief sketch of your life as a *nisei* and *kibei*?
A: How shall I start? Well, I will give you some of my childhood experiences, is that OK? I was born in 1920 so I am going to be seventy-three this year. I grew up in a family where both parents were *isseis*, from Fukuoka prefecture, and I had five brothers and a sister. One of my brothers passed away in his infancy. I was number two of the boys and below me I had three brothers, including the one who died, and one sister above me.

When I was 10 years old I was sent back to Japan with my kid brother and spent my time there, almost ten years. I left Hawai'i in 1930 and came back in 1939, just before the War started. When I first went to Japan I lived with my mother's mother who was a very strong believer in Jodoshinshu, and I was brought up by her, so her influence on me was very, very great. She made me what I am today, I think.

Q: It is characteristic of the *nissei* generation that they had no grandparents, because the grandparents were back in Japan. But you had.

A: I was very fortunate to be able to go back to Japan and live there. It was in the country and in those days we did not have such a thing as television. Today there is a lack of communication in the families because we all watch television. But in my childhood we did not even have a radio and the only way to spend an evening was to have a conversation going. In my case I only had my grandmother and the age gap was quite big. She living in one world and I living in another. Yet, as we communicated at night around the *hibachi*, you know, I started to learn a lot of things. I was the only person, a boy, but she looked on me as a man, the man of the house, because her husband was dead. You know, in Japan, men are always in the front. They represent the family. So whenever there was a party, for example, my grandmother, instead of going, said, 'You are the man in the family and you must go.'

Q: Even though you were only 10-15?

A: That's right. So I went and when I came home she would ask if it was fun and I had to tell her about all the people at the party. Then she would tell me all the stories about the family members, so I got to know the various people quite well. As I was the youngest at these parties, the others in the family remembered me and really took care of me. So I learned much. Also my grandmother would say that she would like to go to this and that temple, but she had a cold, so would I? Would I go and listen to the sermons and come home and tell her what I heard from the minister?

And this is what happened one time. I went to this temple to the *goshoki* (ho-onko), which you know is the very important service, Shinran Shonin's memorial service in November. So I went to this temple because my grandmother was ill, but yet her heart was there. She gave me, I think, one yen and that was big money in those days. Maybe she also kind of bribed me, you know, so I went. This was when I was in my first year in high school. Anyway, I sat among all the old folks, listening to something I just couldn't understand. But at the end this minister, the guest speaker, closed his speech with one poem. And it really took me. I have forgotten the exact words, but it was about this Zen monk who was cleaning the yard in autumn. He was trying to rake up all the fallen leaves and clean up the place, and he picked up the last leaf and thought everything was done. He decided to go to his temple, but when he looked back, he saw that there were another 2-3 leaves fallen behind him. That scene the speaker read in the poem and tying it in with his sermon. I was really taken by this and felt like a saint, felt purified and fresh. Yet when I came out of the temple and there was somebody I could not find or my shoes were not right there, I felt that somebody had stolen them. Just a few seconds before you felt that everything was clear, but as soon as you come out you start developing feelings. That was what the speaker was trying to read into the poem. But, do you know my grandmother? I said to myself that I had to remember the poem, so I jotted it down when I came home. When my grandmother asked me about the lecture, I answered that I could not understand a thing of what he said, but in the last part he read out this poem – and then I told her the poem. To this she said, 'Now this is exactly how I am.' I didn't understand what she really meant, but she said, 'This is me.' So I said, 'Obaasan, how can it be about you? I cannot see any fault in you? And you try to tell me you are not good?'

But as the years have gone and considering the little education she had, it is quite incredible how much she knew. She knew most of the popular sutras by heart. She picked all her knowledge up attending these temple services.

□

Another story: When I and my brother went back to Japan my mother gave me an *o-mamori*. I happened to lose that in the toilet at school, and in such a dirty place that I did not want to pick it up. But when I came home, I said to myself that I had better go and get it, before I got some kind of punishment. I had a fever and was lying in bed because the teacher had sent me home. The reason why I lost the *o-mamori* was I had had a terrible stomach and wanted to go to the toilet which the teacher allowed me to. That was when I lost my *o-mamori*. In the evening I felt better and thought I would go back to the school and pick it up, but when I told my grandmother she told me, 'You did not drop that intentionally. Don't go. There is no god or buddha that will try to punish you, they have nothing but compassion.' The way she put it made me feel so glad. That is how she guided me.

When I came back to Hawai'i, it was then the War started. At that time I had three brothers back in Japan. Also my mother was in Japan, because she had gone there with my father's ashes and wanted to come back after the memorial service, but the War started and she was stranded there. And I was living with my oldest brother here. Naturally, I was investigated by the FBI and the Navy Intelligence. Several times I went to their offices when they called me. During the War I was working on the waterfront for a trucking company. Because we were to go in and out of the harbour, we had to have a special licence. Because of my background, the FBI took it away from me, so I couldn't continue my job.

Some of the questions I was asked were quite difficult. Some were like those you hear of in history like stepping on a *fumie* ('pictures to step on', Christian figures used during the Edo period to identify adherents of Christianity). The same question I was asked. 'You, David Kobata, say you pledge your loyalty to the United States. Can you prove it to me by stepping on the Emperor's picture?' So I was quite upset for a moment, but said, 'Oh, yes, I will, but under one condition.' So they said, 'What is the condition?' 'You lay down President Roosevelt's picture on the floor and you step on that, too. If you do, I will step on the Emperor's picture.' 'Why do you want that?' he said. I said, 'Even though it is President Roosevelt's picture, I don't believe that you are going to be disloyal to the President. How can you take it as a proof that if I step on the Emperor's picture I am proving my loyalty to my country America?' They let me go, but when I came out of the office I had cold sweat, because I thought that if this was in Japan and I had said that, I think I would be dead by now. But, I said to myself, this is America. They respect the freedom of speech. That is a very good thing about the United States.

One time they asked me, if Japanese troops came to Hawai'i after taking over all the South Pacific islands, if I should face my brother (one was old enough for that and one might volunteer), would I then kill my brothers? I said to them, 'Could I wait and answer that question when the time comes?' 'Why?' they said. 'Well,' I said. 'If he wants to kill me, I must protect myself. But as much as possible, as he is my brother, I will not kill him.'

In the end they let me go and didn't send me to a Concentration Camp. I was not interned. When the War ended, lots of my friends returned from these camps. But I was classified as 4-A, that is 'dangerous character'.

My wife is also a *nisei*, born on Maui, and a *kibei*. She came from Hiroshima on the last boat before the War broke out.

Text 45

Daniel K. Inouye: '*You Dirty Japs*'

*D*aniel K. *Inouye, politician of Japanese descent, elected US Senator in 1962 for the Democratic Party, gives his reaction to what happened on 7 December 1941.*

D an Inouye, a senior at McKinley High School, got on his bicycle to go to the aid station at Lunalilo School. He saw frightened people out on the streets and wondered what would become of them.

> They had worked hard. They had wanted so desperately to be accepted, to be good Americans. And now, in a few cataclysmic minutes, it was all undone, . . . And then, pedalling along, it came to me at last that I would face that trouble, too, for my eyes were shaped just like those of that poor man in the street, and my people were only a generation removed from the land that had spawned those bombers, the land that sent them to rain destruction on America, death on Americans. And choking with emotion, I looked up into the sky and called out, 'You dirty Japs!'

> Why had they done it? Why couldn't they let us live in peace? My mind reeled with tormented, confused, unanswerable questions. Once, with the sharp pain of a fresh wound being freshly plucked, it came to me that any one of the men in that armada of planes flaunting the rising sun could be my cousin, and to this day I do not know but what it might have been so, for I have never wanted to find out.

Inouye, Daniel K.
Journey to Washington, p. 56-57

(*Okage Sama De* – *The Japanese in Hawaii*,
ed. by D.O. Hazama & J.O. Komeiji,
(Bess Press, Honolulu, 1986)), p. 125

Shin Buddhist Mission in Hawai'i – an Interview

Interview with Rinban (Head Priest) Fukuhara Hosen, Higashi Honganji, on 6 February 1993.

Q: Would you give me a brief sketch of your life?

A: I was born in Ishikawa ken in Japan on 8 May 1927. My father passed away last October at the age of 84. It was very sad for us. But I was brought up in Ishikawa, a farming land, until I graduated from high school and then, as the eldest son of the family, and the one to take over the temple, I was sent to Otani University. I didn't really know what to study. But one day I met Professor Kenryu Kanamatsu who was teaching Western philosophy. He started out with the question, 'Has anybody thought of what man is?' So I thought that this professor is different from other professors. He was teaching Plato's and Socrates' philosophy and I was very fascinated and started learning Greek. I was very fortunate to study the dialogues in the original. The main theme was 'to know oneself'. Besides that I was taking Buddhism and other types of philosophy. I took my master's degree and continued to study the old Greeks with the help from Prof. Kanamatsu.

After that I worked for a short while for the head temple, Higashi Honganji, guiding visitors and foreigners around the temple, explaining things to them. I was also in charge of receptions when important people from all over Japan visited us.

In 1963 the Abbot Ohtani asked me if I would like to go to Hawai'i. In 1960 a tidal wave had taken away the Hilo Higashi Honganji on the Big Island. Much of Hilo town was destroyed and many people had died. Fortunately, the urns of the dead members of the congregation were saved in a corner of the temple. We were afraid that it was the end of the temple, but we began to rebuild it listening to the teachings of the nembutsu. I said to the Abbot, 'OK, I will try.' So I came over to Hawai'i in 1963, in November.

When I arrived John F. Kennedy had just been assassinated, a very sad coincidence. When I went to Hilo the congregation started to build the temple on a new piece of land. We went from house to house to ask for donations so we could buy materials and build ourselves. The building itself was done by all the members.

It took me about ten years to pay the debts of the temple. After ten years I went home but everything had changed. It was very difficult to adjust to the way of living back home in Ishikawa ken. During the next five years I also went abroad. To Los Angeles to the dedication ceremony of the new betsuin there, and to Chicago. But then I was asked by the former bishop of the Honolulu betsuin to take over his place as he was getting old. The temple then was two blocks down from here and was in a bad shape full of termites. The roof was leaking and when it rained we had to put buckets, even in the altar. So we had to rebuild - either at the same site or at a new place.

It was 1979 I took over and started looking for the possibilities of relocating the temple. Fortunately, the former owner of this land had grandparents who used to come to the temple and they said that if the owner wanted to sell his place, he should ask the temple first. We paid about 800,000 dollars and that meant that we had to pay interests of about 5000 dollars a month. For the building we had all kinds of ideas, also more Oriental architecture, but that was too expensive.

With the help from many people we were able to finish the new building in 1983. Then there were new difficulties. I was reassigned back to Hilo, many ministers moved around, but eight years ago I was reassigned to the betsuin, especially to work for the Dobokai movement in Hawai'i. It is a small group. 5-6 members from each of the six temples in Hawai'i get together to study Shin Buddhism through the Meditation Sutra. We hope to accomplish our studies in another three years.

But we have language barriers in Hawai'i. Some ministers cannot speak English well, while some do.

Q: How would you characterize the situation of the mission in Hawai'i?

A: We have many denominations within Buddhism in Hawai'i. We have Hongpa Honganji and Higashi, which follow the same teachings of Shinran Shonin. Others are Soto, Tendai, Shingon, Nichiren and Jodo. Higashi has a history of 95 years of missionary work. The families are still coming to the temple. In the Honolulu area we have four temples: the betsuin, Palolo, Kaneohe and McCully. McCully has a nisei minister who unfortunately is sick now. He had a stroke not long ago. We used to have young local born people coming into the ministries, but it is very difficult since we cannot pay them the way they are paid elsewhere. Ours is a way of poverty.

Q: So nowadays you get ministers from Japan?
A: Unfortunately, we have to depend on Japan, on the headquarters to send us new ministers from time to time. But it is very difficult to keep them because eventually they will want to return to Japan to take over their fathers' temples. While the parents are healthy, they can stay in Hawai'i, but when the parents are getting old they have to return. Of course they have a chance to become American citizens here, and I am one of them. I became an American citizen 25 years ago, and as my son is here, I would like to stay in Hawai'i the rest of my life. Earlier, I wished to go back all the time, but I am getting settled down here. It is OK. Whereever you are, that is the centre of the world. However, to compare with other denominations, the Hongpa Honganji is the biggest. Next Jodo, Soto, and Higashi, more or less the same size. Then Tendai and Nichiren. Hongpa is trying its best to give teaching in English. They have about one dozen local born ministers.

We have about 2000 members in all, but including the families we are bigger. In the betsuin we have over 500 members, associate members, but regular paying members are not too many. Still, we send out about 500 newsletters every month.

Since I was away eight years ago, somehow we dropped the Sunday school because of language problems. But it is our task from now to recruit younger members. From this year I have started a Sunday school again and so far a couple of kids have started to come. We will combine our Sunday school with that in McCully, Kaneohe and Palolo and take turns. We can do something, outings, sports, handicrafts and something. Of course, when the members come here for memorial services, burials, weddings, we try not to speak Japanese. However, some older folks say it is easier to understand Buddhism in Japanese. But the younger generation say they don't understand any Japanese. They look like a Japanese, but they are not Japanese. We are caught in between.

Q: Are all the parts of a service in English?
A: The chanting of the sutras we do in the same way as in Japan, but the letters of Rennyo (Ofumi) and the sermons are in English. We have regular services every Sunday.

Honolulu Betsuin, Higashi Honganji

Palolo Honganji

Q: Weddings you perform. What about the presentation of infants?
A: Only very few times, according to the requests of the family. We then tell the family how important the religious education is, right from the beginning of life. But it is not a regular thing. In connection with Shinran Shonin's birthday ceremonies in April, though. But not at all like the Christian baptizing. It may, however, be a good idea to bring in more young people to the temple.

Q: What about the kikyoshiki, do you perform that?
A: In the past the Abbot and the Abbots family used to come around and then they performed the confirmation rites. I was also asked to perform the confirmation rites by the Waimea temple on the Big Island. So we wrote a letter to headquarters, in connection with some anniversary. But so far we never performed any. Somebody could come from Japan to do it. It is important. Of course some go to Japan to get the rites, but for those who cannot go, we should provide it here with the honzan's understanding.

Q: Is it part of the plans in your Dobokai group to go the the Dobokaikan in Kyoto?
A: Maybe after the three-year plan they should go to Japan, because it is very important for the members to go to Japan to stay together with others at the Dobokaikan, to listen to the teachings and confirm themselves as Buddhists. They may have language problems, though.

I myself have been educated at the Dobokaikan and have met members from all over Japan. I also have cleaned the floor in the Founder's Hall at Susu-harai. It was a good experience.

Q: At the Dobokaikan the average age is about 53-54. It it the same here?
A: The same age. The young people are too busy earning their money.

Q: I have met the attitude in Japan: Maybe the young people are not as religious as we could wish, but they are busy and may have a hard time making out. So, it is all right. They will come when they get older. Is that an attitude you recognize?
A: Well, we should not neglect approaching younger people, but they are so preoccupied.

Q: But you cannot force them?

A: No, they will come when the time is ripe.

Q: How do you look upon the future of Buddhism in Hawai'i?
A: When I was young, I had hundreds of Sunday school children. Now there are so many things going on and it is much more difficult to get young people back to the temple. Today is very different from 30 years ago. Of course they come to memorial services for their grandpas and grandmas. It is important for us to give the teachings in simple language so they may understand. It is our task to deliver the simple story and experience of Buddhism in English so they may not lose the way. Well, we are not chasing after them or forcing them. Until the time is ripe, you know, it is up to each individual. That is the way of Higashi Honganji, I believe. We don't push people, we don't sell people fortune papers or do other strange things to attract people.

Text 47

Oshogatsu – New Year's Day

O f the many cultural customs the old Japanese New Year celebrations have been chosen as an example of change and continuity among the Hawai'ian Japanese.

M any Japanese families in Hawai'i continue to celebrate New Year's Day in a modified traditional manner. A few do so with an understanding of the reasons for the different customs, but most follow the customs because they had observed their parents doing so.

Over the years, some of the practices have changed. Sometimes it was because of the unavailability of materials. At other times it was a melding of the practices from the different prefectures. The influence of the non-Japanese can be seen especially in the foods. In spite of the changes, recent visitors from Japan have been heard to say that the Japanese in Hawai'i celebrate New Year's more traditionally than do the Japanese in Japan today. The Hawai'i Japanese continue to follow the customs of the Meiji era that the early immigrants brought with them.

The Japanese see the New Year's as the opportunity to begin the year with a clean slate. Debts are paid, quarrels are settled, houses are cleaned, baths are taken, and new clothing is worn for the occasion. They also believe that the New Year brings good luck. In Hawai'i the Japanese have adopted the Chinese custom of burning firecrackers to welcome the luck. They are reluctant to sweep away the residue because it would mean sweeping away the luck.

Beginning with New Year's Eve, many go to the temples and shrines. The Shinto shrines are especially popular at this time of the year. People may be seen in long lines waiting their turn to receive the blessing. The first ritual is for the worshipper to wash his hands and to rinse his mouth at the special basin located just inside the *torii* gate. He then goes up a few steps towards the main shrine where he receives a cleansing from the priest who sprinkles water over him from a leafy branch. The priest also waves a wand of white prayer papers to bless the worshipper. The people sip *sake*, receive amulets, and donate money.

Not only are the houses cleaned, but special decorations symbolizing positive characteristics are set up. A few families use the traditional *kadomatsu* (gate pine) ornament at the doorway. Three stems of bamboo with their ends cut at a slant are arranged with two kinds of pine, a rough bark and a smooth bark, which are tied together. In Hawai'i most families purchase bundles of pine and bamboo branches and use them instead. The bamboo represents great strength coupled with gentleness while the evergreen pine signifies constancy and longevity. It is believed that families displaying the *kadomatsu* will live long and happy lives.

A New Year's offering, *osonae*, of two *mochi*, a strip of *konbu*, and a citrus is placed over *saiwai-gami* (happiness paper). The *saiwai-gami* depict one or all of the seven gods of good luck or symbols representing them. The *mochi* represent the sun and the moon. The smoothness and the roundness of the *mochi* signify harmony. The seaweed, *konbu*, is used because it sounds like a part of the word for happiness, while the citrus is placed because the Japanese word for a kind of citrus is *dai-dai*, which also can mean generation to generation. Sometimes dries persimmons are placed alongside for health and success. Osonae are put in honoured places around the house.

Another ornament is the money tree. In old Japan, temple worshippers were given bamboo stems with miniature good luck symbols. Among the symbols are a treasure boat, a sea bream, a gold coin, a money box, a die, a fan, and a target and arrow. Today plastic 'branches' may be purchased and displayed.

Mochi (rice cake) is a must at New Year's. Although most families today buy their *mochi*, there are still some who gather a few days before the first of January to pound their own. A special kind of rice is soaked overnight, then streamed in square wooden trays over an outdoor stove. The rice is then put into a wooden or cement mortar and pounded with long-handled wooden mallets. In between the pounding, another person turns the rice over, timing the motion so his hand isn't hit. When the rice becomes smooth and elastic, it is transferred to a table where others break off small clumps and shape them. Sometimes small balls of sweetened beans are put in the centres.

A must at breakfast on New Year's Day is *ozōni*. For this dish toasted mochi is put into a broth along with other ingredients such as vegetables and fish. The kind of broth and the accompanying ingredients except for the *mochi* vary from prefecture to prefecture. *Mochi* is eaten for strength and for family cohesiveness. Sometimes youngsters vie with each other to eat *mochi* equivalent to their ages.

During the day friends, neighbours, and families call on each other. In recent years, the all-day open house has changed to lunch or dinner. Special food known as *osechi ryōri* is served. Musts are *kuromame* (black beans), *kazunoko* (herring eggs), *konbumaki* (seaweed roll), *kinton* (mashed sweet potato and chestnut), and *kamaboko* (fish cakes). There is a reason for each dish. *Kuromame* is for health, *kazunoko* for fertility, *konbumaki* for happiness, *kinton* for wealth, and *kamaboko* for happiness and luck. Besides the *osechi ryōri*, Hawai'i tables are graced with turkey, ham, fried noodles, salad, *sushi* (rice rolled in seaweed), *nishime* (vegetables cooked in stock), *sashimi* (raw fish), and cooked red fish. The number of dishes as well as the number of items in each dish must be odd numbered, but never nine.

(*Okage Sama De – The Japanese in Hawaii*
ed. by D.O. Hazama & J.O. Komeiji,
(Bess Press, Honolulu, 1986), pp. 263-65)

Text 48

Haneda Nobuo: *The Future of Shin Buddhism in America*

*H*aneda Nobuo is an important scholar and conveyor of Shin Buddhism to the West who works for the Numata Center for Buddhist Translation and Research, Berkeley, California.

We see – or at least we hope to see – three forms of Shinshu Buddhism in America.

(1) Japanese Shinshu (i.e., the Buddhism of the *issei*, which uses the Japanese language.)
(2) Japanese-American Shinshu (i.e., the Buddhism of the *nisei*, which uses both Japanese and English.)
(3) American Shinshu (i.e., the Buddhism of the *sansei* and of some other Americans, which uses English.)

At present (1989), the *sansei*'s average age is nearing forty. This means that we are moving from stage (2) to stage (3).

Although Shinshu temples in America need to make radical changes in the way they present the Shinshu, they still preserve the Buddhism of stage (1). For example, sutras are chanted in classical Japanese in spite of the fact that most of the congregation don't understand what they mean. In consequence, the *sansei* are turning their backs on Buddhist temples. Thus Buddhist temples are in a serious institutional crisis. Two forms of Shinshu Buddhism already exist in America. But can (3) American Shinshu exist here? Many people are asking this question.

Generally speaking, the religious activities of Shinshu temples in America fall into two categories:

(a) Funeral ceremonies, memorial services
(b) Educational activities such as studying Shinran Shonin's teaching

At present, the main function of the temple is performing (a); (b) constitutes only a very small part of temple activities. Although (a), which is based on the cult of ancestor worship, is important for the *issei* and the *nisei*, it has little meaning for the *sansei*. Interracial marriages are coming among the *sansei*; they are part of the American mainstream. For mainstream Americans, the main function of a religious institution is not performing rituals for the dead, but teaching a religion which is meaningful to their lives.

So whether there can be an American Shinshu depends solely on whether Shinshu temples can outgrow their 'funeral home' function and become educational institutions. The Shinshu Buddhism which has been imported from Japan must be critically scrutinized; its ethnic elements (which have meaning only for the Japanese) must be differentiated from its universal elements (which have meaning for everyone).

While interest in (a) is waning, interest in (b) is gradually increasing. A number of people have started to investigate the universal meaning of the Shinshu from both a religious and an academic standpoint. This makes me think of the importance of Rev. Manshi Kiyozawa (1863-1903), a famous Shinshu teacher. He considered the universal question 'What am I?' the central issue in the Shinshu. His emphasis on the universality of the Shinshu exerted a considerable influence on many Buddhists in Meiji Japan. I believe that he will play an important role in American Buddhism.

Lastly, I wish to discuss what hinders the development of American Shinshu. We have certainly encountered various difficulties in introducing the Shinshu to a different culture. But in my opinion, the greatest hindrances do come, not from American culture, but from Japanese and Japanese-American attitudes. For example, the strong sectarianism which we see among Japanese Buddhists and the ethnocentric attitude towards Buddhism which we see among Japanese-Americans are great obstacles to the development of American Shinshu. Unless they are transcended, Shinshu will become a historical relic recorded on one page of Japanese-American history.

I believe the Shinshu as revitalized by Rev. Kiyozawa will keep on shedding its light in America. To be sure, the number of Shinshu temples will decrease. But I am not pessimistic. In a sense, this is a good process. It raises the crucial question, 'What is the real Shinshu?' In the future, lifeless elements in Japanese Shinshu will be abandoned and forgotten. But vital elements will take root in the new soil of America and keep on growing.

The historical challenge that we are now facing is enormous. We must grasp the essence of Shinshu: self-examination. It is deep understanding of the self that has universal meaning for everybody in the world. If we truly bring Shinran Shonin's teaching into our lives, we can share it with other people.

The 5th World Dobo Convention (Higashi Honganji)

Text 49

Rev. Ryo Imamura:
Excerpt from a Sermon

Rev. Ryo Imamura, grandson of the most outstanding Shin Buddhist priest in Hawai'i, Bishop Yemyo Imamura (1866-1932), Honpa Hongwanji, thinks of Buddhism as a spiritual support to social change. In 1972 he and others established the Buddhist Study Center in Hawai'i whose aim is to tell the public about Buddhist history, culture and thinking.

Comparatively speaking, Honolulu isn't nearly as polluted as some of the other places I've lived in the past few years. But it's no lie when I say that we are catching up to the problems of more polluted cities and catching up fast. How often have you heard the remark, 'Wow, has Honolulu changed!' from someone who had been away for a few years. That remark is very rarely a compliment. He's probably referring to our skyline of instant high-rise buildings, our roads which are just as congested as those of any major city, our sprawling growing suburbs, the neon signs, the roar of jet airliners, and the odour of carbon monoxide fumes.

Here are a few statistics compiled by the City and County of Honolulu for the year 1970:

1. 1,700 tons of impurities discharged into air of Oahu each day; 69 per cent caused by automobiles.
2. Over 340,000 vehicles registered in Oahu for 630,000 people. Less than 2 people (children included) per car.
3. Each resident of Oahu produces an average of 7.8 pounds of refuse a day.
4. Sewage is 103 million gallons per day and more than half is discharged into the ocean untreated.

5. We are gradually but surely losing our hearing. Many Honolulu residents cannot even hear the buzz of a mosquito. And to think that there's an African tribe whose members speak in whispers and can hear a mosquito at twenty feet.

I assume that we can go on from this point with the consensus that we do indeed have ecological problems here in Honolulu. Now how can we relate Buddhism to the current environmental dilemma?

The Buddhist teaching which points out to us the interrelatedness of man and nature, of all forms of life, provides us a solution to the ecological crisis. For, if man understands the interrelatedness and interdependence of man and nature, he would feel deeply responsible for the welfare of the world and be more wise and compassionate in his attitude and actions towards all of mankind and nature. All forms of life have a common essence – Buddha-nature. To do harm to one form of life is essentially to do harm to oneself as well. Plants and animals (man included) live in a balanced relationship with their environment. Nature is a force that demands retribution from all who disturb the balance and harmony of the environment. Man has disturbed and continues to disturb the balance of nature either intentionally or through sheer ignorance. Man is reaping his reward in respiratory troubles, chemical poisoning, deafness, extinction of various forms of animal and sea life, the disappearance of trees, and overpopulation.

Pollution is a man-made problem and it is becoming increasingly clear that we cannot live with it much longer. We must either solve it or suffer because of it. To solve it, man must realize his oneness with Nature, his interdependence with Nature, and be more responsible for his attitudes and actions towards the world.

(*Kodomo no tame ni – For the sake of the children – The Japanese American Experience in Hawaii*, ed. by Dennis M. Ogawa (University of Hawai'i Press, 1989), pp.552-54)

Text 50

K.P.Kramer & K.K.Tanaka: *Excerpt from a Buddhist-Christian Dialogue*

If only for its geographical position Hawai'i is an ideal centre for East-West studies, among these the dialogue of religions. The periodical 'Buddhist-Christian Studies', published by the University of Hawai'i, is central for this dialogue. Mr Kramer is a Professor of Religion at San Jose State University, and Mr Tanaka is a Shin Buddhist priest working at the Institute of Buddhist Studies, Berkeley, California.

KRAMER: From Jōdo-Shinshū perspective, what is the meaning of Death? If you do not look beyond death, is it the final termination of human consciousness?

TANAKA: To answer that, I think we need to go back to the original objective of the *Dharma*, the elimination of suffering. That's the 'monkey on your back'. But that, according to Shinshū, is resolved in the experience of *Shinjin* in this life. Once this is realized, there is a total sense of interconnectedness, a sense of being embraced by the other-power or the greater reality which we call 'Amida Buddha'. How to describe that experience is a separate question. In a modern context I think you say it is finding a oneness with all beings and that is the soteriological solution. So it is no longer a question of what happens to my body or me. This is not a significant concern. Of course, doctrinally we say that upon death one attains full enlightenment, full Buddhahood. In this life one attains complete assurance of becoming a Buddha upon death.

KRAMER: But what does it mean to say, at death you become a Buddha?

TANAKA: Buddha as in the sense of totally overcoming one's existential suffering which initiated the spiritual journey. Then the question of what happens to me as an ontological or physical being is less of a significant concern. Shinran told his followers that upon his death, they should throw his body into the river and let the fishes feed on it.

KRAMER: Of course. At death I throw my body into the ground and let the worms feed on it. But isn't there a striking similarity here between the Christian and the Jōdo-Shinshū view of afterlife? Don't Jōdo-Shinshū parishioners look forward to becoming a Buddha after death?

TANAKA: Yes; however the question of what happens is tied to another question: What is Buddhahood? That question does not lead the one who has realized *Shinjin* faith to ask, 'What happens to me after I die', or 'Where am I going?' or 'What is going to happen to me?' These are secondary concerns compared to the *Shinjin* awareness or insight in *this* life. The whole problem was his attachment to the idea of a separate self. When that conception has been eliminated, then one awakens to this interconnectedness and *that* itself is the soteriological transformation.

KRAMER: What about those whose *karma* in this life is so evil, so self-centred, that upon death they would be too impure to become Buddha?

TANAKA: There is a way out of that, for Jōdo-Shinshū teaching is meant specifically for those whose *karma* is woefully inadequate. It is not your *karma* that brings about Buddhahood or enlightenment but the Vow Power (or the Other Power) of Amida Buddha (the *symbol* of Suchness or Absolute Reality) being transferred to the spiritual seeker. For those endowed (by Amida) with the pure mind of *Shinjin* faith, they are assured of attaining Buddhahood immediately after death.

KRAMER: What is it, or is there anything about Christianity, the knowing of which would assist you in being a Buddhist.

TANAKA: The immediate issue that comes to my mind is the involvement or participation in history which I believe that Buddhists have not emphasized as Christians have. And so for that reason it helps me to actualize that dimension of benefiting others, the Bodhisattva dimension. And in Shinshū we have a term, *gensō*, which means 'returning' from the Pure Land. The essence of this means that the realization should not only be for yourself, but that one has to return into the realm of *saṃsāra* to lead others. The Christian concern for greater involvement in society and history helps to remind me of the Bodhisattva tradition of selfless giving (*dāna*) that has, perhaps, been de-emphasized.

KRAMER: Obviously Christ on the cross is the paradigm of suffering for Christians. Christ literally chose that suffering, he brought suffering upon himself. One could even say, that he saw it to be the only way to affect history, that is through human suffering. But not in the Buddhist sense of a self-transformed, self-realized, self-actualized person who is no longer personally attached to the suffering, yet who is identified with all human suffering. Look at the Buddha's life. I'm not aware of instances, aside from his death, of Buddha's suffering. His is more an enlightenment story, a story of compassion for all sentient beings. In Jesus' story, on the other hand, he is depicted as one who suffers. This whole issue of physicality means that history and suffering go together in the Christian view.

In the New Testament there is constant reference to suffering as the way in which the Christian's faith matures. Here of course we can agree that *faith* is what saves/liberates us. We cannot do it ourselves. It comes from the other. Yet in the Christian tradition in order to access the power of the other, suffering is a primary condition if for no other reason than suffering forces the sufferer to realize how dependant he or she is on other-power.

TANAKA: So there is a sense of enduring the difficulties of life-situations?

KRAMER: Yes, identifying with the suffering of the world is the way a Mother Teresa might put it. How can I be a joy-filled Christian when I know that right outside of this building, someone is suffering, let alone right inside this building. What good is salvation, if I attain it by myself? None!

TANAKA: Okay; I think that is a good point. There is in Buddhism the Bodhisattva ideal with such a sense of sacrifice. There is the sort of a Bodhisattva meeting a tigress and a cub who is hungry. And so he offers himself as food. So there is that kind of sacrificing and identifying with someone else's plight. The Bodhisattva ideal exists within the tradition but, institutionally, it has not been adequately emphasized. The exemplars are extraordinary people, and perhaps that's the problem for they have attained heights far beyond the reach of ordinary Buddhists to identify with. So, they are exceptional Buddhists. In Christianity, perhaps even the ordinary, unenlightened people are called to identify more with suffering. Another point is that some Buddhists believe that some Christians are primarily intent on making everyone like themselves. So a Christian concern for others can sometimes be misinterpreted by some Buddhists as self-aggrandizements or self-propagation, a Christianizing of the world. Some Buddhists have used that as a cop-out for not being more socially involved. But such apathy is contrary to the true spirit of the Bodhisattva ideal.

(K.P. Kramer & K.K. Tanaka, 'A Dialogue
with Jodo-Shinshu', *Buddhist-Christian
Studies* (1990), pp. 182-84)

Text 51

Esben Andreasen: *Overview – Tensions in Shin Buddhism today*

In the various chapters of this introduction to Shin Buddhism there are certain issues that sum up the predicaments of the religion today. Foremost among these issues are the ones that reveal a gap between folk beliefs and theology, a tension which has a very long history in Shin Buddhism.

The *locus classicus* is the conflict between Kakunyo (1270-1325), the great-grandson and biographer of Shinran, and Kakunyo's son, Zonkaku (1290-1373), over the question of funeral rites. Kakunyo quoted Shinran for the following attitude towards death and memorial rites: 'When I shut my eyes for good, you must throw my body in the Kamo river (in Kyoto) as food for the fish' and Kakunyo concluded: 'On reflection it follows that we should not consider services for the dead as all-important but rather put an end to them.' Zonkaku, who was disowned by his father and denied leadership in the main temple, is very important for reconciling Shinran's teaching with traditional patterns of Japanese religious thought and practice. About memorial services he wrote: 'One must not neglect the monthly services for the deceased, and certainly not the yearly observances on the anniversary of the dead. Even after many years have passed, on these anniversaries one must absolutely lay aside one's worldly affairs to pray for the peace of these souls.'

Many theologians today consider Zonkaku's Shin Buddhism, of which ancestor worship is only a part, as a betrayal of Shinran's true faith and a compromise with folk religion, and they prefer Kakunyo's rationalist approach. However, ancestor worship is not a dividing issue in Shin Buddhism today (see Chapter Six on

'Death and Burial in Shin Buddhism') but many other folk religious practices are, as can be seen in the same chapter in the interview, Text 37. Such issues concern 'hungry spirits' (*gaki*) and ceremonies for dead children (*mizuko kuyo*), which theologians call 'superstition'. The difficulty is to reconcile or balance the demands of 'household religion' and the orthodox teachings of Shin Buddhism.

In the eighteenth century discussion of the conditions for 'peace of mind' (*anjin*) or Buddhist salvation one group of Shin theologians claimed that belief in Amida should be expressed in 'three kinds of acts' (*sango*), viz. thought, word and action. But another faction argued that the one mind of entrusting Amida would ensure *anjin*, and the latter party won the day in the so-called Sango Upheaval (*sango wakuran*). In this dispute lies buried the same conflict between a puritan outlook of 'faith only' and a more popular type of Shinshu life including religious rites. Again, there may not be any deep conflict between 'faith' and 'deeds' in ordinary Shin congregations today, but the most important modern reformer of Shin Buddhism, Kiyozawa Manshi, almost polemically advocates the way of 'entrusting' (see Text 8) and so do the university-educated theologians.

Of course, the great challenge to Shin Buddhism after World War II has been the New Religions in Japan. They are in many respects at the other end of the religious spectrum with belief in spirits, excorcism and a great number of rites to ensure 'this-worldly benefits' (*genze riyaku*), i.e. the belief that already in this life you find the results of your religious endeavours. Over the years many Shin Buddhists have crossed over to these New Religions, to some analysts because Shin Buddhism has rejected these very popular and very Japanese beliefs. Perhaps the most important element in the New Religions is the reliance on and important role of laymen, and to meet the challenge of organizing the laity both Nishi and Higashi Honganji have set up lay organizations (see Chapter 3). As with the questions regarding ancestor rites, the art of balance is to teach the laymen what is considered true Shin Buddhism and at the same time accommodate the 'household religions' of the Shin Buddhist believers. The present situation in Higashi Honganji, indicated in the introduction to Chapter 3, of a possible split between the Otani family and the main temple, also contains a tension between popular and theological Shin Buddhism because of the way ordinary Shin believers have looked up to the Otani family. Matters concerning the Otani family are connected with the role of the Founder of Shin Buddhism, a role that is given almost divine dimensions among the believers.

The above-mentioned tensions are the most important in the present introduction to Shin Buddhism, but of course there are others incorporated in the texts. (And some, for example the role of women in Shin Buddhism and the role of Shin Buddhist leaders in World War II and before, are not even mentioned.)

That these tensions give rise to genuine concern among Shin Buddhists is indicated by the fact that they are included in a debate in Nishi Honganji on how to bridge the gap between the theologians and the laymen. And much concerning the future success of Shin Buddhism in keeping its believers and attracting new members depend on the outcome of the tension. The new reformers, who have started the debate, find encouragement among ordinary temple priests to advocate a 'theology of the founder cult', a 'theology of this-worldly benefits' and a 'theology of ancestor cult'. Incidentally, 'this-worldly benefits' (*genze riyaku*) is not completely foreign to Shin Buddhism: Shinran himself wrote 'Hymns on Benefits in the Present' (*Jodo Wasan*).

Prof. Alfred Bloom

Postscript – An Appraisal of Shin Buddhism in the Modern World

Jodo Shinshu or Shin Buddhism is a tradition some 800 years in development. It was transmitted to the West initially through the immigrant Japanese people who came to work on sugar plantations in Hawai'i or to seek their fortunes in other occupations beginning in the late nineteenth century. It is found chiefly in Hawai'i and on the west coast of the North American mainland, as well as in Brazil and Peru in South America. Small congregations can be found scattered over the continent as a result of dispersion in the Second World War. Being largely ethnic in character, it has not been as well known as Theravada, Tibetan or Zen traditions in the West.

Its basic approach to spiritual emancipation or deliverance stresses faith and the recitation of the name *Namo Amida Butsu* as an expression of gratitude for the deliverance offered by Amida Buddha through his Primal Vows. It has been a major, popular faith in Japan and for this reason has often been dismissed by scholars and religious seekers as a simplistic faith for people incapable of deeper understanding of Buddhist teaching. It calls itself the easy path, which has a technical meaning in the Buddhology, but has sometimes been interpreted by Westerners as a do-nothing religion. It has also shared in the ceremonial emphasis on the dead with funerals and memorials, because of its background in Japanese concern for ancestors. It appears highly other-worldly.

Nevertheless, despite its traditional forms which have been transmitted to modern times, the teachings of the founder Shinran are oriented towards life in this world. With the arising of faith and certainty concerning one's final fulfilment in the Pure Land, the focus of concern is on living in this world with confidence and compassion, sharing the teaching and maintaining positive social relations within the society where one lives.

Although religious practice does not include formal practices of meditation or prayers, the recitation of name inspires deep self-reflection on the compassion one has received and an awareness of one's human limitations and weaknesses. It works to bring about a transformation in attitudes, behaviour and value priorities. Sharing in the broader Mahayan Buddhist philosophy, it enables the person to realize fundamental Buddhist insights which alter one's ordinary way of looking at life and people. Consequently, through reflection, it leads to the equanimity, peacefulness and positive outlook on life which one may achieve through other forms of Buddhist meditation, despite the fact there are no formal requirements to engage in meditation. It also leads to the formation of a community of fellow companions in the faith (*dobo-dogyo*) who work together for the betterment of humanity through their religious faith.

Although the transition of the institutions of Shin Buddhism to Western culture and the acculturation of the Japanese-American community has created tensions and problems within the organization, the meaning and vitality of the teaching remains as a resource for personal and social renewal. With increased reading materials, translations of major texts, study programmes and study centres, as well as increased participation in the wider religious environment beyond the temples, leaders and members are increasingly becoming more aware and sensitive to the deeper meanings of the teachings and the issues in our contemporary culture. Consequently, the movement has a rare opportunity to present the views of Shin Buddhism to a sympathetic audience and to engage in friendly, but realistic dialogue, in Western culture. Particularly through Buddhist-Christian dialogue programmes in academia, as well as in local churches, interfaith understanding is increasing.

To the question: 'What can Shin Buddhism offer to Western people?', we would point to several aspects that make it a worthy alternative for religious seekers.

The teachings emphasize deliverance through Other Power, which has affinity with Christian teaching. However, this does not mean that a God, a power outside the self, bestows deliverance, but that the power becomes manifest within the self in a new view of life, taking seriously the principle of interdependence and one's solidarity with all beings. These principles are manifested within the story of Amida's Forty-eight Primal Vows which express in dramatic form the interdependence and indivisibility of deliverance.

Secondly, Shinran recognized that religion itself may be a danger to one's spiritual development. The belief that one can achieve enlightenment through one's own efforts, one's own striving, leads to comparisons, self-righteousness and the elitism that infects all religions (including later Shin Buddhism). Shinran's view of Other Power altered the understanding of religious life by transforming it from a religion of self-perfection or self-benefit to a religion of gratitude and commitment. Religious faith became an end in itself and not a tool or means to some other end. For Shinran, one becomes religious because one is aware of the compassion that embraces one's life and expresses it in gratitude and sharing. The essence of religious faith is altruism. One lives to convey compassion to others.

Thirdly, Shinran overcame the manipulative, oppressive, religious fears that attend Japanese folk religion and is also present in various forms in Western religious tradition. He noted that the gods bow down and worship the person of trust rather than people being fearful of angry spirits or deities and supplicating them. In this he was in line with a long tradition in Buddhism which has been often overshadowed by Buddhism's own involvement in folk religious practices. He is important in our day to counteract the uncritical, often frenetic, or fanatic, adherence to religious leaders claiming some special religious status or powers. Shinran never claimed to be anything more than a stubble-haired common person, neither a priest nor a layman. He was not legalistic or authoritarian.

Fourthly, within the Western context, Shinran's understanding of Amida is a significant alternative to belief in God as it has been developed in Christian tradition. Rather than a self-existent, Creator God, separate from the creation and the world of human beings, Amida in contrast may be viewed as a 'deconstructed God'. He symbolizes cosmic compassion and wisdom and the life force which brings us to enlightenment without the substantialist, metaphysical, objectivistic implications of traditional Christian theology. Amida is a religious symbol in the deepest sense of the term symbol, which focuses our spiritual vision on the ontological implications of our own being, that we cannot live without interdependence, caring, community, or compassion and love in some measure. Amida is realized as the depth of our existence.

The recitation of his name, as an element of devotion, is not magical, but a means to focus our attention on the deeper reality of our life. Our language about Amida appears theistic, but anthropomorphism is involved in religious expression universally, because the human person is the highest reality that we know. However, Buddhism warns us not to identify substantively our human conceptions, generated through egoistic concerns, with the ultimate nature of reality which is beyond conception and speech. Where Christianity, as a result of its history, became cosmological in orientation, Buddhism, particularly Shin, is ontological. Buddhism and Shin do not intend to make a statement about the nature of the world, but to offer a perspective for evaluating life, human relations and the meaning of existence.

The philosophical background of Shin Buddhism lies in the non-dualistic Mahayan Buddhist tradition. In this context, Shin overcomes the rigid distinctions in Western religion and Islam between flesh and spirit, sacred and secular, and science and religion.

Finally, Shinran's teachings offer a comprehensive understanding of religious existence with a cosmic-universal view of reality, a deep understanding of the condition of the self, a basis for religious experience and a foundation for meaningful existence. It can be a source for healing in society. Its realistic view of self embraced by unconditional compassion inspires self-acceptance and its correlate acceptance of others. It is a faith of reconciliation, transcending socially imposed distinctions, creating a fellowship of companions on the way. Shinran's teaching does not support repressive, competitive, moralistic, legalistic or authoritarian attitudes and structures in religion. It opposes exploitive, oppressive religious beliefs and practices, offering freedom from religious fears and removes the basis for ego-aggression rooted in certain types of religious beliefs. Shinran's way in modern society has the potential to bring healing to a fragmented and despairing world, if his spirit can become real within the community that proclaims his teaching.

ALFRED BLOOM
Professor Emeritus
Department of Religion
University of Hawai'i

Notes on the Readings

The list below gives the sources for all the texts, except those written especially for this book by the author. It gives the name of the author, the title of the original work and the publisher.

Chapter 1: Shinran – the founder

1. Lady Yoshiko Ohtani: *Eshin-ni – the Wife of Shinran Shonin*, pp. 31-32, 34.(Honpa Hongwanji, Kyoto, 1969-70). Reprinted by permission of Hongwanji International Center, Kyoto.

3. *Tannisho: A Primer*, translated by Dennis Hirota, pp. 22, 23-24, 37-39. (Ryukoku University, Kyoto, 1991). Reprinted by permission of Dennis Hirota.

4. *Mattosho – Letters of Shinran*, pp. 19-20, 22-24, 60-62. (Shin Buddhism Translation Series, Hongwanji International Center, 1978). Reprinted by permission of Hongwanji International Center.

5. *Kyogyoshinsho – the True Teaching, Practice and Realization of the Pure Land Way*, Vol. 1, pp. 160-167. (Hongwanji International Center, 1983). Reprinted by permission of Hongwanji International Center.

Chapter 2: Shin Buddhism in the Modern Age

6. *The Skeleton of a Philosophy of Religion*, by Prof. M. Tokunaga (Kiyozawa Manshi), pp. 2-5. (Kawai Bunkodo, Tokyo, 1893).

7. *December Fan – the Buddhist Essays of Manshi Kiyozawa*, pp. 37, 41-42. (Higashi Honganji, Kyoto, 1984). Reprinted by permission of Higashi Honganji.

8. *December Fan – the Buddhist Essays of Manshi Kiyozawa*, pp. 57-60. (Higashi Honganji, Kyoto, 1984). Reprinted by permission of Higashi Honganji.

9. *Shout of Buddha – Writings of Haya Akegarasu*, pp. 90-92. (Orchid Press, Chicago, 1977). Reprinted by permission of Gyoko Saito, Higashi Honganji Buddhist Temple, Los Angeles.

10. *Shout of Buddha – Writings of Haya Akegarasu*, pp. 167-68. (Orchid Press, Chicago, 1977). Reprinted by permission of Gyoko Saito, Higashi Honganji Buddhist Temple, Los Angeles.

11. 'Dharmakara Bodhisattva', by Soga Ryojin, *Eastern Buddhist*, Vol. 1, No. 1

(1965), pp. 64-66, 78. Reprinted with permission.
12. 'Shin Religion as I Believe it', by Kaneko Daiei, *Eastern Buddhist*, Vol. 8, No. 2 (May 1951), pp. 40-42. Reprinted with permission.
13. *Collected Writings on Shin Buddhism*, by D.T. Suzuki, p. 51. (Shinshu Otaniha, Kyoto, 1973). Reprinted with permission.
14. *Collected Writings on Shin Buddhism*, by D.T. Suzuki, p. 57-61. (Shinshu Otaniha, Kyoto, 1973). Reprinted with permission.
15. *Collected Writings on Shin Buddhism*, by D.T. Suzuki, p. 117. (Shinshu Otaniha, Kyoto, 1973). Reprinted with permission.
16. *Lectures on Shin Buddhism*, by Hirose Takashi, pp. 47-51. (Higashi Honganji, Kyoto, 1980). Reprinted by permission of Higashi Honganji, Kyoto.

Chapter 3: The Dobokai Movement
17. *The 6th World Dobo Convention*, pp. 57-58. (Higashi Honganji, Kyoto, 1992.) Reprinted by permission of Overseas Section of Higashi Honganji, Kyoto.
18. ('*Manual for Propagators of the Dobokai Movement*'), pp. 4-8. Dobokaikan, Higashi Honganji, Kyoto, 1992. Translated from the Japanese by Prof. Aasulv Lande, University of Lund, Sweden.

Chapter 4: Shin Buddhism and the Arts and Crafts
20. *Shinran – an Introduction to His Thought*, by Yoshifumi Ueda and Dennis Hirota, pp. 291-294. (Hongwanji International Center, 1989). Reprinted by permission of Hongwanji International Center.
21. *The Ten Foot Square Hut and Tales of the Heike*, tr. by A.L. Sadler (1928), pp. 1, 19-21. (Tuttle, Tokyo, 1990).
22. *Year of My Life – a Translation of Issa's Oraga Haru*, tr. by Nobuyuki Yuasa, pp. 139-140. (University of California Press, 1960). Reprinted by permission of University of California Press.
23. *Haiku*, Vol. 1, by R.H. Blyth, pp.303-304. (Hokuseido Press, 1981). Reprinted by permission of Hokuseido Press.
24. *The Autumn Wind*, tr. by Lewis Mackenzie, pp. 5,7 and 90. (Kodansha, 1990). Reprinted by permission of Kodansha International Ltd.
25. *Japanese Spirituality*, by D.T. Suzuki, tr. by Norman Waddell, pp. 182-183. (Japan Society for the Promotion of Science, 1972). Reprinted by permission of Norman Waddell.
26. 'The Dharma Gate of Beauty', by Yanagi Soetsu, *Eastern Buddhist*, Vol. 12, No. 2 (Oct. 1979), pp. 5-6, 15-16. Reprinted with permission.
28. *The Buddha Tree*, by Niwa Fumio, pp. 193-195. (Tuttle, 1989). Reprinted by permission of Peter Owen Ltd., London.

Chapter 5: Rituals in Shin Buddhist Temples – notably Higashi Honganji

Chapter 6: Death and Burial in Shin Buddhism
34. *Hikkei – Shinshu Jibutsu no Kaisetsu*, ('Handbook – Explanation on Shinshu Matters'), by Nishihara Hoshun, 1978. Translated from the Japanese by Prof. Yasutomi Shinya, Otani University.
35. *The Shinshu Seiten: The Holy Scripture of Shinshu*, The Honpa Hongwanji Mission of Hawaii, 1978, (originally published 1955), p. 377.

Chapter 7: Shin Buddhist Education
38. Translated by Prof. Aasulv Lande, University of Lund, Sweden.

Chapter 8: Shin Buddhist Mission in Hawai'i
42. *Okage Sama De - The Japanese in Hawaii*, by D.O. Hazama & J.O.Komeiji, pp. 63-64. (Bess Press, 1986). Reprinted by permission of Bess Press, Honolulu.
43. *Memoirs of a Buddhist Woman Missionary in Hawaii*, by Kikuchi Shigeo, pp. 34-38. (Buddhist Study Center Press, Honolulu, 1991). Reprinted by permission of the Buddhist Study Center, Honolulu.
45. *Okage Sama De - The Japanese in Hawaii*, by D.O. Hazama & J.O.Komeiji, p. 125. (Bess Press, 1986). Reprinted by permission of Bess Press, Honolulu.
47. *Okage Sama De - The Japanese in Hawaii*, by D.O. Hazama & J.O.Komeiji, pp. 263-65. (Bess Press, 1986). Reprinted by permission of Bess Press, Honolulu.
48. *The 5th World Dobo Convention*, Higashi Honganji, Kyoto, pp. 34-35. (Higashi Honganji, Kyoto, 1989). Reprinted by permission of Dr. Nubuo Haneda.
49. *Kodomo no tame ni - For the Sake of the Children - The Japanese American Experience in Hawaii*, ed. by Dennis M. Ogawa, pp. 552-554. (University of Hawai'i Press, 1989, originally 1978). Reprinted by permission of University of Hawai'i Press.
50. 'A Dialogue with Jodo-Shinshu', by K.P. Kramer and K.K. Tanaka, *Buddhist-Christian Studies*, Vol. 10, 1990, pp. 182-184. (University of Hawai'i Press, 1990). Reprinted by permission of Prof. David W. Chappell and Prof. K.P. Kramer.
51. Overview: For the Nishi Honganji debate referred to in the text, see Sasaki Shoten, 'Shinshu and Folk Religion - Towards a Post-Modern Shinshu 'Theology'', *Nanzan Bulletin 12* (1988).

Bibliography

Abe Masao, ed., *A Zen Life: D.T. Suzuki Remembered* (Weatherhill, 1986)

Akegarasu Haya, *Selections from the Nippon Seishin* (Kososha, 1936)

Akegarasu Haya, *Shout of Buddha* (Orchid, Chicago, 1977)

Andreasen, Esben, Ian Reader & Finn Stefansson, *Japanese Religions – Past and Present* (University of Hawai'i Press, 1993 & Japan Library 1993)

Becker, Carl, 'Pure Land Buddhism in Christian America', *Buddhist-Christian Studies*, vol. 10 (1990)

Bellah, Robert, *Tokugawa Religion – the Cultural Roots of Modern Japan* (The Free Press, 1985) (originally 1957)

Bellah, Robert, 'The Contemporary Meaning of Kamakura Buddhism', *Journal of the American Academy of Religion*, vol XLII, 1 (March 1974)

Berentsen, Jan-Martin, *Grave and Gospel* (University of Oslo, 1982)

Bloom, Alfred, 'The Life of Shinran Shonin – the Journey of Self-Acceptance', *Numen*, vol. XV, 1 (1968)

Bloom, Alfred, *Tannisho – a Resource for Modern Living* (Buddhist Study Center, Hawai'i, 1981)

Bloom, Alfred, *Shoshinge – the Heart of Shin Buddhism* (Buddhist Study Center Press, Hawai'i, 1986)

Bloom, Alfred, *Shinran's Gospel of Pure Grace* (University of Arizona Press, 1987)

Bloom, Alfred, 'The Unfolding of the Lotus: A Survey of Recent Developments in Shin Buddhism in the West', *Buddhist-Christian Studies*, vol. 10 (1990)

Blyth, R.H., *Haiku*, vol. 1 (Hokuseido Press, 1992)

Chomei, Kamo no, *The Ten Foot Square Hut*, tr. by A.L. Sadler (Tuttle, 1990)

Coates, Harper Havelock & Ryagaku Ishizuka, *Honen – the Buddhist Saint* (Chion-in, 1925)

Conze, Edward, tr. & ed., *Buddhist Texts Through the Ages* (Shambhala, 1990)

Conze, Edward, *A Short History of Buddhism* (Oneworld, Oxford, 1995)

Cooke, Gerald, 'The Struggle for Reform in Otani Shin Buddhism', *Japanese Religions*, vol. 10, 2 (July 1978)

Cooke, Gerald, 'A New Life-Stage in the Otani Denomination', *Japanese Religions*, vol. 15, 3 (Jan. 1989)

Corless, Roger Taishi, 'Shinran's Proofs of True Buddhism', *Buddhist Hermeneutics*, ed. by Donald S. Lopez (Motilal Banarsidass Publishers, Delhi, 1993)

Davis, Winston, *Japanese Religion and Society* (State University of New York Press, 1992)

de Bary, William Theodore, ed., *The Buddhist Tradition in India, China and Japan* (Vintage, 1972)

Dobbins, James C., *Jodo Shinshu: Shin Buddhism in Medieval Japan* (Indiana University Press, 1989)

Dobbins, James C., 'Women's Birth in Pure Land: Intimations from the Letters of Eshinni', *The Eastern Buddhist* (New Series), Vol. XXVII, No. 1 (Spring 1995)

Dumoulin, Heinrich, *Understanding Buddhism – Key Themes* (Weatherhill, 1994)

Dumoulin, Heinrich & John C. Maraldo, *Buddhism in the Modern World* (Collier, 1976)

Earhart, H. Byron, *Japanese Religion – University and Diversity* (Wadsworth, 1982)

Fox, Douglas A., 'Soteriology in Jodo Shin and Christianity', *Contemporary Religions in Japan*, vol IX, 1-2 (March-June, 1968)

Franck, Frederick, ed., *The Buddha Eye – an Anthology of the Kyoto School* (Crossroads, 1982)

Fujita Kotatsu, 'The Origin of the Pure Land', *The Eastern Buddhist*, Vol. 29, No 1 (Spring 1996).

Gœmez, Luis O., *Land of Bliss – Sanskrit and Chinese Versions of the Sukhavativyuha Sutras* (University of Hawai'i Press & Higashi Honganji Shinshu Otani-ha, Kyoto, 1996)

Hanayama Shoyu, *Buddhist Handbook for Shin-shu Followers* (Hokuseido Press, 1969)

Harrison, Elizabeth G., 'Mizuko kuyo: the re-production of the dead in contemporary Japan', *Religion in Japan – Arrows to heaven and earth*, ed. by P.F. Kornicki and I.J. McMullen (Cambridge University Press, 1996)

Hayami Tasuku, 'On Problems Surrounding Koya's (Kuya's) Appearance', *Japanese Religions*, Vol. 21, No. 1 (January 1996)

Hazama, Dorothy Ochiai & Jane Okamoto Komeiji, *Okage Sama De – The Japanese in Hawaii* (Bess Press, Honolulu, 1986)

Hirose Takashi, *Lectures on Shin Buddhism* (Higashi Honganji, 1980)

Hirota, Dennis, tr. and ed., *No Abode – the Record of Ippen* (Ryokoku University, 1986)

Hirota, Dennis, tr. and ed., *Plain Words on the Pure Land Way – Sayings of the Wandering Monks of Medieval Japan* (Ryukoku University, 1989)

Honen, *Selected Sayings of St. Honen* (The Jodoshu Press, 1977)

Honpa Hongwanji, *Shin Buddhist Handbook* (Honpa Honganji Mission of Hawai'i, 1972)

Honpa Hongwanji, *Shinshu Seiten* (Honpa Honganji, Hawai'i, 1978)

Hori Ichiro, *Folk Religion in Japan* (University of Chicago Press, 1974)

Hunter, Louise, *Buddhism in Hawai'i: Its Impact on a Yankee Community* (University of Hawai'i Press, 1971)

Inagaki Hisao, *A Dictionary of Japanese Buddhist Terms* (Heian International, 1989)

Inagaki Hisao, ed., *The Three Pure Land Sutras – a Study and Translation* (Nagata Bunshodo, Kyoto, 1994)

Ippen, *No Abode*, tr. by Dennis Hirota (Ryukoku University, 1986)

Issa Kobayashi, *The Autumn Wind* (Kodansha, 1990)

Issa Kobayashi, *The Year of My Life* (University of California Press, 1960)

Joji Okazaki, *Pure Land Buddhist Painting*, translated and adapted by Elizabeth ten Grotenhuis (Kodansha 1977)

Kanamatsu Kenryo, *Naturalness* (Bummeido Press, 1978)

Kaneko Daiei, 'The Buddhist Doctrine of Vicarious Suffering', *The Eastern Buddhist*, Vol. IV, No. 2 (July – Aug – Sept 1927)

Kaneko Daiei, 'Shin Religion as I Believe it', *The Eastern Buddhist*, Vol. VIII, No. 2 (May 1951)

Kaneko Daiei, 'The Meaning of Salvation in the Doctrine of Pure Land Buddhism', *The Eastern Buddhist* (New Series), Vol. 1, No. 1 (Sept. 1965)

Kaneko Daiei, 'Two Thinkers on Shin', *The Eastern Buddhist* (New Series), Vol. XXVII, No. 1 (Spring 1995)

Kaneohe, Higashi Honganji, *Service Book* (Hawai'i)

Kashima Tetsuden, *Buddhism in America – the Social Organization of an Ethnic Religious Institution* (Greenwood Press, 1977)

Kashiwahara Yusen & Sonoda Koyu, eds., *Shapers of Japanese Buddhism* (Kosei, Tokyo, 1994)

Keel, Hee-Sung, *Understanding Shinran: A Dialogical Approach* (Asian Humanities Press, 1995)

Ketelaar, J. E., *Of Heretics and Martyrs in Meiji Japan* (Princeton, 1990)

Ketelaar, J. E., '*Kaikyoron*: Buddhism Confronts Modernity', *Zen Buddhism Today*, No 12 (March 1996)

Kikuchi Shigeo, *Memoirs of a Buddhist Woman Missionary in Hawai'i* (Buddhist Study Center Press, Hawai'i, 1991)

Kishimoto Hideo, ed., *Japanese Religion in the Meiji Era* (Obunsha, 1956)

Kiyota Minoru, 'Buddhist Devotional Meditation: A Study of the *Sukhavativyuhopadesa*', *Mahayana Buddhist Meditation – Theory and Practice*, ed. by Minoru Kiyota (Motilal Banarsidass Publishers, Delhi, 1991)

Kiyota Minoru, 'Buddhism in Postwar Japan – a Critical Survey', *Monumenta Nipponica*, vol. XXIV, 1-2 (1969)

Kitagawa, Joseph M., *Religion in Japanese History* (Columbia University Press, 1966)

Kitagawa, Joseph M., *On Understanding Japanese Religion* (Princeton University Press, 1987)

Kiyozawa Manshi, 'A Skeleton of a Philosophy of Religion', *Kiyozawa Manshi Zenshu*, vol II (originally 1892)

Kiyozawa Manshi, *Selected Essays* (Bukkyo Bunka Society, 1936)

Kiyozawa Manshi, *December Fan* (Higashi Honganji, 1984)

Kleine, Christoph, 'The *Separate Biography* of Honen: A Translation and Critical Analysis of the *Betsu-denki*', *Japanese Religions*, Vol. 21, No. 1 (January 1996).

Kotani, Roland, *The Japanese in Hawai'i – a Century of Struggle* (The Hawai'i Hochi, 1985)

Kramer, Kenneth P. & Kenneth K. Tanaka, 'A Dialogue with Jodo Shinshu', *Buddhist-Christian Studies*, vol. 10 (1990)

Kubose Gyomay M., *Everyday Suchness* (Dharma House, Chicago, 1967)

Kubose, Gyomay M., *The Center Within* (Heian International, California, 1990)

LaFleur, William, *The Karma of Words – Buddhism and the Literary Arts in Medieval Japan* (University of California Press, 1983)

LaFleur, William, *Liquid Life – Abortion and Buddhism in Japan* (Princeton, 1992)

Lloyd, Arthur, *The Creed of Half Japan* (London, 1911)

Lopez Jr., Donald S., ed., *Buddhism in Practice* (Princeton University Press 1995)

Maida Shuichi, *The Evil Person – Essays on Shin Buddhism* (Higashi Honganji North American Translation Center, 1989)

Maida Shuichi, *Heard by Me* (Frog Press, California, 1992)

Matsunaga Daigan & Alicia, *Foundation of Japanese Buddhism*, vol. 2 (Buddhist Books International, 1976)

Minami, Kirsten Gottfredsen, 'The Development of the Karma Concept in Shinran's Thought', *Florilegium Japonicum – Studies Presented to Olof G. Lidin on the Occasion of His 70th Birthday*, Bjarke Frellesvig og Christian M. Hermansen, eds. (Akademisk Forlag, Copenhagen, 1996)

Morioka Kiyomi, *Religion in Changing Japanese Society* (University of Tokyo Press, 1975)

Morrell, Robert E., *Early Kamakura Buddhism – a Minority Report* (Asian Humanities Press, California, 1987)

Mullens, Mark R, Shimazono Susumu & Paul L. Swanson, eds., *Religion and Society in Modern Japan* (Asian Humanities Press, 1993)

Murakami Shigeyoshi, *Japanese Religion in the Modern Century* (University of Tokyo Press, 1983)

Nakai Gendo, *Shinran and his Religion of Pure Faith* (Shinshu Research Institute, 1937)

Nakano Ryoshun, *Self and Society – a Buddhist View* (Higashi Honganji, 1987)

Nishi Hongwanji, *Shinran in the Contemporary World* (Honganji International Center, 1979)

Nitschke, Günter, *Japanese Gardens* (Taschen Verlag, 1993)

Niwa Fumio, *The Buddha Tree* (Tuttle, 1989)

Ogawa, Dennis M., *Kodomo no tame ni – For the Sake of the Children* (University of Hawai'i Press, 1978)

Ohtani Yoshiko, *Eshin-ni – the Wife of Shinran Shonin* (Honpa Hongwanji, 1969-70)

Osumi Kazuo, 'Buddhism in the Kamakura Period', *The Cambridge History of Japan*, vol. 3 (Cambridge University Press, 1990)

Otani Kosho Konyo, *The Successor – My Life* (Buddhist Books International, 1985)

Pilgrim, Richard B., *Buddhism and the Arts of Japan* (Anima Publications 1993)

Reader, Ian, *Religion in Contemporary Japan* (Macmillan, 1991)

Rhodes, Robert F., 'Pure Land Practitioner or *Lotus* Devotee? The Earliest Biographies of Genshin. *Appendix*: Translation of the *Kakocho* Biography, *Japanese Religions*, Vol. 21, No. 1 (January 1996)

Rhodes, Robert F., 'A New Approach to Medieval Pure Land Buddhism: Taira Masayuki, *Nihon chusei no shakai to Bukkyo*' (Review article), *Japanese Religions*, Vol. 21, No. 1 (January 1996).

Reischauer, August Karl, *Studies in Japanese Buddhism* (AMS Press, 1970)(opr. 1917)

Rennyo, *Words of St Rennyo*, tr. by K. Yamamoto (Kavinbunko, 1968)

Rogers, M.L. & A.T. Rogers, 'The Honganji: Guardian of the State (1868-1945)', *Japanese Journal of Religious Studies*, vol. 17, 1 (1990)

Rogers, M.L. and A.T., *Rennyo – the Second Founder of Shin Buddhism* (Asian Humanities Press, California, 1991)

Sansom, G.B., *Japan – a Short Cultural History* (Tuttle, 1973)

Sasaki Gessho, *A Study of Shin Buddhism* (Eastern Buddhist Society, 1925)

Sasaki Gessho, 'What is the True Sect of the Pure Land?' *Eastern Buddhist*, vol. 1, 3 (Sept.-Oct. 1921)

Sasaki Shoten, 'Shinshu and Folk Religion – toward a Post-Modern Shinshu

Theology', *Nanzan Bulletin 12* (1988)

Shinran, *The True Teaching, Practice and Realization of the Pure Land Way*, vols. 1-4 (Hongwanji International Center, 1990-92)

Shinran, *Tannisho – a Primer*, tr. by Dennis Hirota (Ryukoku University, 1991)

Shinran, *Hymns of the Pure Land* (Hongwanji International Center, 1991)

Shinran, *Hymns of the Pure Land Masters* (Hongwanji International Center, 1992)

Shinran, *Letters of Shinran – a Translation of Mattosho* (Hongwanji International Center, 1978)

Shojun Bando, 'D.T. Suzuki and Pure Land Buddhism', *Eastern Buddhist*, vol. XIV, 2 (Autumn 1981)

Smith, Robert J., *Ancestor Worship in Contemporary Japan* (Stanford University Press, 1974)

Soga Ryojin, 'Dharmakara Bodhisattva', *The Eastern Buddhist* (New Series), Vol. I, No.1 (1965)

Soga Ryojin, 'The Core of Shin', *Japanese Journal of Religious Studies*, Vol. 11, Nos. 2-3 (1984)

Soga Ryojin, 'Two Thinkers on Shin', *The Eastern Buddhist* (New Series), Vol. XXVII, No. 1 (Spring 1995)

Suzuki, Beatrice Lane, *Mahayana Buddhism* (Mandala/Harper Collins 1992) (first publ. 1938)

Suzuki, D.T., *The Lankavatara Sutra – a Mahayana Text* (SMC Publishing, Taipei, China, 1994) (orig. 1932)

Suzuki, D.T., *Mysticism – Christian and Buddhist* (Harper and Brothers, New York, 1957)

Suzuki, D.T., *Shin Buddhism* (Harper & Row, 1970)

Suzuki, D.T., *Japanese Spirituality* (Ministry of Education, Japan, 1972)

Suzuki Daisetz Teitaro, *Collected Writings on Shin Buddhism* (Shinshu Otaniha, 1973)

Suzuki Daisetz, 'Shinran's World' (1) *The Eastern Buddhist (New Series)*, Vol. XVIII, No. 1 (Spring 1985) (Dialogue with Soga Ryojin, Kaneko Daiei, and Nishitani Keiji)

Suzuki Daisetz, 'Shinran's World' (2) *The Eastern Buddhist (New Series)*, Vol. XIX, No. 1 (Spring 1986) (Dialogue with Soga Ryojin, Kaneko Daiei, and Nishitani Keiji)

Suzuki Daisetz, 'Shinran's World' (3) *The Eastern Buddhist (New Series)*, Vol. XXI, No. 2 (Autumn 1988) (Dialogue with Soga Ryojin, Kaneko Daiei, and Nishitani Keiji)

Suzuki, D.T., 'Zen and Shin', *The Eastern Buddhist (New Series)*, Vol. XXVII, No. 1 (Spring 1994) (Dialogue with Soga Ryojin)

Suzuki, David A., *Crisis in Japanese Buddhism – Case of the Otani Sect* (Buddhist Books International, 1985)

Takahatake Takamichi, *Young Man Shinran – a Reappraisal of Shinran's Life* (Wilfrid Laurier University Press, 1987)

Tannisho Kenkyokai, *Perfect Freedom in Buddhism* (Hokuseido Press, 1968)

Terakawa Shunsho, 'Shin Buddhism in Modern Japan: An Examination of the Thought of Manshi Kiyozawa', *Studies in the History of Buddhism* (B.R.Publishing Corporation,. Delhi, 1980)

Thelle, Notto R., 'Power Struggle in Shin Buddhism: Between Feudalism and Democracy', *Japanese Religions*, vol. 9, 3 (Dec. 1976)

Umahara Takeshi, 'The Philosophical Characteristics of Japanese Buddhism',

Florilegium Japonicum – Studies Presented to Olof G. Lidin on the Occasion of His 70th Birthday, Bjarke Frellesvig og Christian M. Hermansen, eds. (Akademisk Forlag, Copenhagen, 1996)

Ueda Yoshifumi & Hirota Dennis, *Shinran – an Introduction to His Thought* (Hongwanji International Center, 1989)

Wanatabe Shoko, *Japanese Buddhism – A Critical Appraisal* (Tokyo 1970)

Weinstein, Stanley, 'Rennyo and the Shinshu Revival', *Japan in the Muromachi Age*, ed. by John W. Hall & Toyoda Takeshi (University of California Press, 1977)

Yamamoto Kosho, *An Introduction to Shin Buddhism* (The Karinbunko, 1963)

Yanagi Soetsu, 'The Pure Land of Beauty', *Eastern Buddhist*, vol. IX, 1 (May 1976)

Yanagi Soetsu, 'The Dharma Gate of Beauty', *Eastern Buddhist*, vol XII, 2 (Oct. 1979)

Yanagi Soetsu, *The Unknown Craftsman* (Kodansha, 1989)

Yasutomi Shinya, 'Japanese Religions – a Buddhist Point of View', (unpublished lecture held at the NCC, Kyoto, Nov. 29, 1988)

Yasutomi Shinya, 'Shinran's Historical Consciousness', *Japanese Religions*, Vol. 21, No. 1 (January 1996)

Yasutomi Shinya, 'The Legacy of Meiji Shinshu', *Zen Buddhism Today*, No. 12 (March 1996)

Young, Richard & Ikeuchi Fuki, 'Religion in "the Hateful Age": Reflections on *Pokkuri* and Other Geriatric Rituals in Japan's Aging Society', *Japanese Religions*, Vol. 20, No. 2 (July 1995)

Zotz, Volker, *Der Buddha im Reinen Land – Shin-Buddhismus in Japan* (Eugen Diederichs Verlag, München, 1991)

Glossary of Japanese Words

Amida	Amitabha Buddha, the most important Buddha of Shin Buddhism
betsuin	main temple in a district
bunkotsu	'part of the bones', referring to the custom of double tombs
butsudan	'Buddha shelf', Buddhist altar in private homes
daimyo	feudal lord
Dobokai	'community of brothers in faith' lay movement at *Higashi Honganji*
doso	temple priest
dotoku	ethics (school subject)
fumie	'pictures to step on'. To identify Christians in the Tokugawa period they were forced to trample on Christian icons.
gagaku	court music
gaki	hungry spirit
genzo	to return, viz. help save human beings
Godensho	'the life', i.e. the life of Shinran, the biography by Kakunyo
gyo	religious austerities, good works
haiku	classic form of poetry consisting of three lines with 5, 7 and 5 syllables
haka mairi	visit to the graves of the ancestors
hanga	wood-print
hibachi	charcoal brazier used as a source of heat
higashi	east
Ho-onko	the annual memorial ceremonies for Shinran

hombyo	original mausoleum
homyo	'dharma name', the Buddhist name given to a person at the time of his initiation as a priest or layman, or at his death
Honganji	'temple of the original vow'
hotoke	a buddha, referring to the popular belief that people become buddhas after death
ihai	memorial tablet with one's name after death placed on the *butsudan*
Ikko Ikki	peasant uprisings by Shin Buddhists in the fifteenth and sixteenth centuries
issei	first generation immigrants
jiriki	'self-power', the belief that one is saved by one's own efforts
jodo	'the Pure Land'
Jodoshinshu	'the True Pure Land School', Shin Buddhism, founded by Shinran
Jodoshu	'the Pure Land School', founded by Honen
juzu	Buddhist rosary
kibei	children of Japanese emigrants sent back to Japan to get a Japanese upbringing
mingei	folk crafts
mizuko kuya	ceremonies performed for dead children or abortions
monshu	Shin Buddhist abbot
monto	pious adherent of Shin Buddhism
myokonin	'wondrously happy man', ideal lay *nembutsu* practitioner in Shin Buddhism
Namu Amida Butsu	'I take refuge in Amida Buddha', the fundamental profession of faith in Pure Land Buddhism
nembutsu	short for *Namu Amida Butsu*
Nichiren Shoshu	Buddhist school founded by Nichiren
Nihongi	'Chronicle of Japan', sacred script in Shinto, written in 720 AD
nisei	second generation immigrant
nishi	west
O-Bon	Buddhist observance honouring ancestor spirits in mid-July (or mid-August)
O-Higan	'the other shore', Buddhist memorial ancestor observances at spring and autumn equinoxes
o-kamisori	ritual tonsure of Buddhist priests and laymen,

195

	also performed at burials
pachinko	popular pinball arcade hall
pokkuri dera	'temple for sudden death', temple visited by the elderly
sambo	'three treasures', 'I take my refuge in the Buddha, the Dharma and the Sangha'
sansei	third generation immigrant
segaki-e	rituals for 'hungry ghosts' (gaki)
shin	'true'
Shingon	school of esoteric Buddhism founded by Kukai
shinjin	moment of belief or conversion in Shin Buddhism
Shinshu	short for *Jodoshinshu*
Shinto	the indigenous religion of Japan
Shogun	military dictator
Shonin	'eminent priest', honourable title
Soka Gakkai	new religion, organization of laymen in *Nichiren Shoshu*, today the connection between Soka Gakkei and Nichiren Shoshu has been dissolved
sorei	'soul', ancestor spirit
sosen suhai	ancestor worship
tamashii	'soul'
tariki	'other-power', i.e. Amida's power to save
temizu	the washing of hands, especially at a Shinto shrine
Tendai	comprehensive school of Japanese Buddhism, founded by Saicho
tokonoma	decorative alcove in private homes
ukiyo-e	coloured wood-print
wagesa	band of cloth worn by Buddhist priests or laymen having undergone religious training
wasan	Buddhist psalms, whose most influential writer was Shinran
zen	Buddhist school, building on meditation as the most important way of gaining salvation

Index